D1558773

JEWISH PERSONAL
& SOCIAL ETHICS

LOUIS JACOBS

Behrman House
West Orange, New Jersey

Library of Congress Cataloging-in-Publication Data

Jacobs, Louis.
    Jewish personal & social ethics / Louis Jacobs.
      p. cm.
    ISBN 0-87441-510-1
    1. Ethics, Jewish. 2. Jewish way of life. I. Title. II. Title:
Jewish personal & social ethics.
    BJ1287.J36   1990
    296.3'85–dc20   90-23131
                                CIP

FOR BASIL AND CORAL SAMUEL

I am deeply indebted to Ms. Kim Fryer, who has exceeded the normal duties of a copy editor in making this book more readable, especially for readers in the USA. And my thanks are due, as always, to Adam Bengal and all at Behrman House. — **LJ**

Published by   Behrman House
                  235 Watchung Avenue
                  West Orange, New Jersey 07052

Design by Seymour Rossel
Typesetting by RCC, Inc.

Contents

CHAPTER 1
Judaism and the Good Life

Ethics

This book is about the Jewish character and the participation of the individual in society. It describes the kind of persons adherents of Judaism should strive to be and the ways they should conduct themselves as members of the Jewish community, the country of which they are citizens, and the world community. The major concern of the book, then, is personal and social ethics.

The Jewish Character

There are few direct references to the ethics an individual should hold in the classical sources of Judaism. A detailed account of how Jewish character should be shaped and expressed is neither possible nor desirable, if only because each individual is unique. What is good and right for one person in a given situation is not necessarily the same for another. If I am overweight, for example, it would no doubt be proper for me to give up the extra cookies which helped lead to my condition, but it does not mean that others should follow my example or that I must continue to be so self-denying once I have achieved a balance between my weight and what I eat. If I am quick-tempered, I would be well-advised to keep my cool even when provoked, but that should not result in total rejection of righteous indignation. And if I feel a need to cultivate a yielding disposition, it does not follow that I am obliged to allow others to treat me as a doormat.

That probably would not be good for me, and it certainly would not be good for others.

That is why there cannot be a *Shulhan Arukh*, a Code of Law, for the cultivation of the ideal Jewish character, as there is, for instance, for food. Obviously, each person makes a choice concerning which of the dietary laws to keep, but the laws themselves are clear on the whole. In the matter of ethics, however, it is difficult to see how there can be hard and fast rules.

No Easy Solutions

There are more detailed rules regarding the life of the Jew in society, but many problems still need to be worked out, because new circumstances, unenvisaged in the Jewish sources, demand a fresh approach. The question, for example, of how best to achieve social justice is far more complicated since the rise of capitalism and organized labor than it was under more primitive economic systems.

This book, therefore, does not purport to provide the impossible: a detailed solution to all of life's problems. I have the far more modest goal of suggesting how the great ethical principles of Judaism can be applied to the individual, drawing upon the work of famous authorities to formulate my own tentative conclusions. I invite the reader to follow my arguments, and, if he or she takes issue with my conclusions, so much the better. Debate and discussion are the only ways to further what is, after all, a quest for the truth.

Although no easy solutions are available, I have tried not to evade the issues. If one is sufficiently foolhardy to write a book such as this, sticking out one's neck cannot be avoided. Writers on controversial subjects often have found the courage to proceed from a statement made by Rabban Johanan ben Zakkai in the Talmud (*Bava Batra* 89b): "Woe to me if I say it; woe to me if I do not." What did he eventually do? Did he say it or not? The Talmud gives the only possible answer: *He said it.*

Broad Principles

Over two-and-a-half thousand years ago, the prophet Micah gave his great prescription for the good life as seen by our religion:

It hath been told thee, O man, what is good,
And what the Lord doth require of thee:
Only to do justly, and to love mercy, and to walk
    humbly with thy God. (Micah 6:8)

The prophet gives us broad principles. God wants us, he says, to be just and fair in our dealings with others, as well as kind and caring. He does not want us to parade our virtues by "showing off." Later Jewish teachings show us how to realize these great principles in our lives. There is, consequently, a wealth of Jewish teachings on how to be just, how to attain a benevolent character, and what it means to walk humbly with God. In the following pages, we shall make frequent recourse to these teachings, but a good deal must be left to individual taste and discretion, especially with regard to the last two.

In addition to numerous laws in the Torah, stories about the lives of Biblical heroes and heroines teach us how to live as Jews. However, they are different from the laws in that they show how men and women struggle with life's challenges and temptations in their own ways. Abraham was not called upon to do what his wife Sarah was. Isaac's role was different from the role of Abraham, his father, just as Isaac's son Jacob had to pursue his own way to obey God. We have the stories to guide us, but, ultimately, we have to tell our own story.

Religion And Ethics

In Judaism ethics are bound up with religion in a way that makes the two inseparable. The good Jew, in the words of the Rabbis, is good both in relation to God and to other people.

The question discussed by thinkers throughout the ages is what is the precise relationship between religion and ethics? Some religious thinkers have argued that religion alone can sustain the ethical life, which means a person without religious belief cannot be "good" in the ethical sense. This view is very hard to sustain. Surely we all know atheists or agnostics who are good to others and "religious" people who are not.

A variation of this argument is that religion determines what is good in the ethical sense: something is good *because* God commands it. Taken to the extreme, this line of reasoning claims it is wrong to steal and right to honor our parents because God said so, but if God had said that we should steal and not honor our parents, that would be the right course to adopt. Such a view seems perverse. A better way of looking at the matter is to say that God, being God, could not possibly have ordered human beings to steal or not to honor our parents. Or to put it simply, a thing is not good because God says so; God says so because it is good. Unless we put it this way, there would be no meaning to the expression used in so many Jewish sources that God is good.

Religion As Another Dimension

Perhaps the most satisfactory way of dealing with the relationship between ethics and religion is to see religion as bringing an extra dimension into human life. When one does not steal, when one honors one's parents, when one practices benevolence and cultivates kindness, one is worshipping God, because these are the ways in which God wishes human beings to conduct themselves. As William Temple once put it, God is interested in many things apart from religion. Our relationship with God is mingled with our relationship with other people. The whole personality is wholesome when it is deficient neither in its relationship to God nor in its relationship to others.

The Imitation Of God

In Rabbinic literature is found the idea that by leading the good life, one is not only obeying God but imitating Him. The well-known Latin expression of this ideal is *Imitatio Dei*.

Deuteronomy 11:22 speaks of "walking in all God's ways." The literal meaning of the verse is walking in the ways that God has ordained. But the *Sifre*, a Rabbinic Midrash, extends the verse to mean that it is desirable for human beings to walk *in the ways that God walks*, to resemble God, to be Godlike. "Just as He is called compassionate, be thou compassionate. Just as He is called merciful, be thou merciful." There could hardly be a more powerful expression of the idea that religion adds an extra dimension to the ethical life.

GLEANINGS

NO TWO EXACTLY ALIKE
The Rabbis taught that whoever sees a large crowd should recite the benediction "Blessed art Thou Who art wise in secrets" (i.e., God knows all the secrets of their hearts). This is because no two faces in the crowd are exactly alike, and just as their faces differ, so do their minds [Talmud, *Berakhot* 58a].

TO BE YOURSELF
A Hasidic master began to depart, in some respects, from the way followed by his father. When the Hasidim objected, the master retorted: "I do follow my father. Just as he departed from the way of his father, I, too, follow in his tradition in departing from his way." Or, as Solomon Schechter remarked, "You cannot get your father to write your love letters for you."

SEEKING FORGIVENESS
Rabbi Eleazar ben Azariah expounded on the verse "From all your sins shall ye be clean before the Lord" (Leviticus 16:30): For transgressions between human beings and God, the Day of Atonement effects atonement; but for transgressions be-

tween human beings and other human beings, the Day of Atonement only effects atonement if the victims are appeased [Mishnah, *Yoma* 8:9].

RIGHTEOUS SINNERS

Hasidim tell of a Rebbe who gave some money to a poor man who was a notorious sinner. "How can the Rebbe give alms to such a man?" the Rebbe's followers asked in surprise. "We are expected," the Rebbe retorted, "to imitate God, and God gives of His bounty to sinners as well as saints. Did he not give the money to me in the first place? I am a sinner."

CHAPTER 2
Self-Improvement

Have We a Duty to Ourselves?

In the Rabbinic scheme, duties are divided into those owed to God and those owed to other human beings. As we have noted, the latter are owed to God as well because God wishes us to behave as decent human beings and thus become whole persons.

The fifteenth-century Jewish philosopher Joseph Albo in his work *Sefer ha-Ikkarim* (Book 3, chapter 25) introduced, like the Christian philosopher Thomas Aquinas before him, a third duty—toward oneself. Other Jewish thinkers following Albo popularized the view that the ideal Jew should have a proper relationship with God by praying regularly and so forth; a proper relationship with others by performing acts of benevolence; and a proper attitude toward self-fulfillment by realizing one's potential. In other words, there are duties to God, duties to others, and duties to the self.

I leave it to the reader to pursue the topic in detail, but it does not seem logical to me to speak of a *duty* to oneself. The notion of duty implies that I have obligations to *another*, whether to God or to other human beings. But how can I have a duty to myself? In what way is the "I" who is said to have the duty different from the "myself" to whom the duty is owed?

Judaism and Self-Realization

Judaism certainly knows the idea of fulfilling one's potential, of realizing the best in oneself. That is surely the meaning of all the admonitions in Jewish literature to be "perfect." But this, too, is part of a person's duty to God. To strive for self-perfection is a religious imperative in Judaism.

Derekh Eretz

The term found most frequently in Jewish literature for ethical conduct is *derekh eretz* ("the way of the land"). It denotes that human beings are *naturally* decent. Since it is the way of the earth, it is the way reasonable people behave. Of course, none of us are reasonable all the time, and it is often a struggle to behave as we should. Otherwise, there would be no need for all the works written to improve one's character.

An Ideal Is an Ideal

Before we examine some of the lofty Jewish teachings on self-improvement, a note of caution should be sounded. These teachings merely point to an ideal, one that is often beyond the normal grasp. It is neither possible nor desirable for everyone to be a saint. Young people, by nature idealistic, sometimes try to make these ideals their own. In this, they are bound to be unsuccessful. They either give up the whole exercise, or they delude themselves that they have reached stages quite beyond them. In seeking to tread the Jewish path to self-improvement, both despair and priggishness must be avoided.

A Question of Balance

In this whole area, a sense of balance is essential if any progress is to be made. The prescriptions for the good life should be seen as high mountains presenting a challenge. So high are these mountains that only a few of the most skillful mountaineers can hope to reach the summit. The rest should try to ascend as high as they can, but should have the good sense to desist from trying to scale heights for which they are ill-equipped. An ideal is precisely that which is unattainable, but this should not result in despair of any hope of improvement. Robert Browning advised: "A man's reach must exceed his grasp or what's a Heaven for?"

GLEANINGS

A DEFINITION
Rabbi Isaiah Horowitz (d. 1630) in his work "The Two Tablets of the Covenant" defines *derekh eretz* as "correct behavior, extraordinary humility, the improvement of the character and all delightful things, to love all creatures and to be loved by them, to be a man of peace and a perfect man, contributing to the world in general and in particular in both worldly and spiritual matters."

PRETENSION
The famous Rabbi Moses Sofer (nineteenth-century) once overheard a man protesting that he was unworthy of the respect paid to him. The Rabbi was irritated and said to the man: "You are not so great that you can afford to be so small."

THE PURSUIT OF HAPPINESS
Rabbi Moses Sofer once observed that a student of his hardly smiled and never seemed to enjoy life. He ordered the student to stop reading moralistic works for a time. "If it makes you so miserable," the Rabbi exclaimed, "there's something wrong with it."

CHAPTER 3
Psychological Unrest
and Peace of Mind

The Good Life as a Struggle

Hardly anyone admits to being cruel, heartless, unfeeling, and self-centered. Practically everyone acknowledges the virtues of benevolence, kindness, generosity, and altruism. Yet there are few who find it easy always to be right in every situation. The businessman who stoops to sharp practices, for example, knows that he is doing wrong, but his self-interest gets the better of him.

There is a constant struggle in the human breast between what we are and what we ought to be. The Rabbis of the Talmud speak of two conflicting impulses in human beings—the *yetzer tov* ("the good inclination") and the *yetzer ha-ra* ("the bad inclination"). The good inclination pulls a person upward, the bad, downward. This Rabbinic concept resembles Freud's analysis of the personality in certain respects. It is suggested in some Rabbinic texts that, until the age of Bar and Bat Mitzvah (13 and 12 respectively), a child is governed by the bad inclination. Freud, too, denies that children are "innocent," although the Rabbis believe that children cannot be held blameworthy for what they do or what they fail to do because of this.

Among Jewish teachers, there are differing emphases on the idea of the struggle between the *yetzer tov* and the *yetzer ha-ra*. Some teachers have a pessimistic view of human nature; for them, people are always in danger of yielding to the demands of their lower nature. Others have a more optimistic view: human beings are naturally good, so comparatively little effort is required to keep them on the right road. Ultimately, it depends upon individual temperament—more is expected from people born with a sunny disposition than from those in whom aggressive instincts are strong. A realistic assessment is to see the struggle taking place in the areas in which an individual is weak.

Peace of Mind

The recognition that the good life is often a struggle ought not to result in a constant taking of one's spiritual temperature or in anxiety that one is failing in the effort to become a better person. A sense of humor and the accompanying sense of proportion are essential for a healthy spiritual approach. Peace of mind is attained through the recognition of one's limitations as well as one's capacities. Rabbi Hayyim Eleazar of Munkacs wisely said, "We read in *Ethics of the Fathers*: 'Judge everyone in the scale of merit.'" That is, give a person the benefit of the doubt; do not judge him or her too harshly. The passage says, "Judge *everyone*," including yourself.

Beside the Still Waters

The Jew who believes that God is in control of His world and makes no excessive demands on His creatures does not become too upset when things do not seem to be going right. In Psalm 23 ("The Lord is my Shepherd"), the Psalmist speaks of God leading him "beside the still waters." The mind of the religious man or woman is quiet and serene even in disturbing circumstances. Life often sours because a man becomes excessively agitated by envy of others whom he imagines are more fortunate than he or because he has an unsatisfied sexual urge or because he has ambitions beyond his ability to realize. As the Rabbis say in *Ethics of the Fathers*: "Envy, lust, and ambition take a man out of his world."

Life's Driving Force

Does this mean there is no room for envy, lust, and ambition in the serene religious life? Surely, these and similar traits are part of human nature; they are the force that makes the world go round. Are we to conclude that the religious Jew should be as indifferent to striving as a Buddhist monk? No. Only *excessive* envy, lust, and ambition are of what the Rabbis speak. The question of sex will be examined in depth later; here all that needs to be said is that Judaism frankly acknowledges that human beings have sexual drives, that God created them with these drives, and, consequently, these are good and contribute to happiness and well-being. When the Rabbis say sex takes a man out of his world, they refer to loss of self-control, when sex is allowed to get so out of hand that it interferes with the other aspects of life.

Envy and Ambition

Judaism teaches that every human instinct must have its place in life, otherwise God would not have created it. While it is true, for instance, that envy of the good fortune of others can poison us and turn life into a rat race, to be envious of the good qualities of others can serve as a spur to emulate them. This is why the Rabbis say that the envy of students and teachers of the Torah increases wisdom. Ambition, too, can be wholesome, provided it does not cause one to disregard the equally legitimate ambitions of others and it does not step beyond its limits. Many people overlook their real talents while trying to fulfill ambitions in areas where they have no abilities. It is useless for a young woman with brains but a poor voice to devote her efforts to becoming an opera singer when, with her brains, she might become a physician or a talented writer. Peace of mind is not attained by forgoing ambition, but by having goals that can reasonably be attained. As the medieval Jewish preacher Jacob Anatoli put it: "If you cannot get what you want, you should want what you can get."

But Is Peace of Mind So Desirable?

A cogent objection to the "peace-of-mind" philosophy is that it tends to encourage indifference to the needs of others. How can a sensitive person fail to be distressed at all the evil things that go on in the world? And in one's personal life, should there not be a strong element of divine dissatisfaction? Rather than an easy acquiescence, should there not be an awareness of the conflict between what one is and what one can become? Like other ideas, the peace-of-mind attitude can be overworked. Again, a sense of balance is required. If peace of mind results from trust in God and a realization that one can only be expected to do one's best, it is not an unworthy attitude. But if it results from a cold calculation that nothing is worth striving for or from a cruel indifference to suffering, then such "peace" is not worth having.

Serious, but Not Too Serious

Reading Jewish moralistic works can be a bit off-putting in that some seem to overstress life's seriousness. One can surmise that the one-sided attitude of the writers of these works is necessary because, as preachers, their aim is to get their message across without including irrelevancies. Nevertheless, the wise student will see the need for relaxation from time to time. Otherwise, studying these works becomes an insufferable burden. To take life seriously, one must not be too serious. This is probably the reason that on Purim it was the practice in the Yeshivot to engage in "Purim Torah," a clever, witty manipulation of Biblical and Rabbinic texts with a strong dose of irreverence.

Of course, the frivolous side must not be overdone; Purim comes but once a year. Yet the good Jew need not be solemn all the time. There ought to be room for hobbies, sports, the cinema, television, vacations, and sheer fun. And piety should never result in a harsh attitude toward others. There is a wonderful story in the Talmud in which Elijah the prophet comes back to earth to conduct a Rabbi on a tour of the community. When the Rabbi asks Elijah which people in the marketplace are guaranteed to go to Heaven, the prophet points to two jesters. "But these are quite ordinary folk," the Rabbi protests. "Yes," replies Elijah, "but whenever these men see someone in distress, they tell jokes and cheer him up. For this alone they deserve a large share in Heavenly bliss."

There is further danger in self–righteousness if one becomes too absorbed in the life of excessive piety. It is not unknown for young men and women who see the light and become *frum* to imagine that they are better Jews than most and to look down on those who do not match their standards. This does not mean that one should not try to be *frum*. But it does mean that one should have a sense of proportion.

The Golden Mean

According to Maimonides, the ideal way to follow is to avoid extremes. A person should not dress in rags, but neither should he or she wear clothing that is too costly. Generosity is admirable, but it should not result in squandering one's resources. One should not be content with bread and water, but neither should one enjoy the best food and the choicest wines. One should avoid taking offense easily, but one is not required to bear every insult without replying. One should not live as a hermit apart from society, but neither should one always be in the company of others. Moderation is called for in all things.

The nineteenth–century Italian scholar Samuel David Luzzatto, known as *Shadal*, was critical of Maimonides' middle way, especially in regard to generosity. The good Jew, *Shadal* argued, should emulate our father Abraham, who knew of no limits to generosity and magnanimity, instead of following an ideal Maimonides had obtained from the Greeks, who thought of the good life as one that was carefully balanced.

It is futile to inquire who is right, Maimonides or *Shadal*. Here, too, it all depends upon circumstances and individual temperament. We can appreciate the value of a balanced, moderate life as taught by Maimonides and yet occasionally wish for a wilder approach, one catering to the need to take risks, to be adventuresome, to be extreme. Even Maimonides advocates following the extreme in one direction for people tempted to do the opposite. For instance, if a man has a niggardly disposition, it is not good for him to try the middle way, Maimonides says, for then he would quickly revert to the extreme his nature demands. To cure himself of his soul's sickness, he must for a time go to the opposite extreme.

GLEANINGS

CHILDREN ARE BLAMELESS
Resh Lakish said in the name of Rabbi Judah the Prince: "The world endures only for the sake of the breath of school children." Said R. Papa to Abbaye: "What about mine and yours?" Abbaye replied: "Breath in which there is sin cannot be compared to breath in which there is no sin" [Shabbat 119b].

LIKE A TREE
A Hasidic master said: "In the Bible human beings are compared to trees. A tree grows if it is healthy, but you cannot watch it grow. So should it be with the human personality. It should grow toward greater perfection, but the growth should be gradual and imperceptible. Too much introspection is morbid."

THE PURPOSE OF ATHEISM
The Hasidic master known as "The Holy Jew" said: "Since everything God created has a purpose, there must be a purpose in atheism. But what can it be? God allows people to doubt His existence," the master said, "so that when it comes to helping the unfortunate, believers should not leave it to God, but behave as if God does not exist and it all depends upon them alone."

MISERY AND JOY

Hasidism teaches that joy (*simhah*) is a great virtue and for a Jew to be miserable, a great vice. But, say the Hasidim, a distinction must be made between misery and bitterness. Misery or melancholy is incompatible with joy, but it is possible and desirable to worship the Lord with joy, yet be bitter at one's remoteness from His truth.

PURIM TORAH

In a *Purimspiel*, Moses, holding a candle, searches for something. "What are you looking for?" he is asked. Moses replies: "I am looking for my original Torah buried under the mass of Rabbinic interpretation."

OWING A GREETING

Rabbi Israel Salanter met a very pious Lithuanian Jew in the period before Rosh Hashana when people engage in severe self-examination. So engrossed was the man in his pietistic exercises that he walked past Rabbi Israel without saying good morning. Rabbi Israel observed: "What right does his piety give him to deprive me of a morning greeting?"

THE FAULT OF FAULTLESSNESS

A shadchan, trying to arrange a match between two young people, extolled the virtues of the young man to the father of the prospective bride. "But what faults does he have?" the father asked. "He has no faults," declared the shadchan. The father indignantly retorted: "To have no faults is the biggest fault of all."

BENDING TO STRAIGHTEN

The commentators on Maimonides' philosophy give this illustration: If a bamboo cane is bent in one direction and you wish to straighten it, simply holding the cane straight is of no use, for it will spring back. You have to bend it in the opposite direction, and then it will straighten.

CHAPTER 4
Humility

The Highest of Virtues

All Jewish teachers consider pride to be one of the worst of faults and humility one of the highest of virtues. In the passage in the Talmud devoted to the evils of the proud and haughty nature, it is said God declares that He and the haughty man cannot live together in the same world and that the man puffed up with pride is abhorrent even to his own wife and family. Concerning humility, the Talmud remarks that the Torah is compared to water; just as water only flows downward, the Torah can only descend from its lofty source into the humble heart and mind.

The attainment of humility is no easy matter. Some fall prey to false modesty, taking a back seat while saying: "See how humble I am." Some may also pretend to be proud in order to delude themselves that they are not guilty of false modesty. Humility does not mean that one overlooks one's worth and attainments. It is absurd, for example, that a great scholar pretend to be ignorant.

Basically, humility is a religious virtue. A believer in God can claim little credit for his or her talents and achievements since these are God's gifts. In Hasidic thought, humility does not mean that one thinks little of oneself, but, rather, one does not think of oneself at all, leading the good life selflessly because God has so ordained. This is an impossibly high ideal for most people. While they may never attain true humility, they can try at least to avoid being proud and arrogant.

In a famous letter, Nahmanides advised his son to be humble by looking upon all men as superior to him. How could he do this? Well, if he met someone more learned and wise, obviously there were no grounds for Nahmanides' son to feel superior. If, on the other hand, the other person was far less learned and not as intelligent, this person may have been a truer servant of God because he or she had to overcome innate disabilities. One might add that almost everybody has a field in which they excel, and it is not delusion to acknowledge inferiority to them in their area of specialty.

Seen in this way, humility is not a contradiction to self-respect. It is only when one feels superior to others and tries to lord it over them that pride becomes, as the Rabbis say, an abomination. There is room for pride in being a Jew, however, in belonging to the people who have sacrificed so much for the sake of God's truth.

GLEANINGS

TWO POCKETS
Said R. Simhah Bunem: "Everyone should have two pockets. In one he should have a slip of paper which reads, 'For my sake the world was created.' In the other, he should have a paper which reads, 'I am dust and ashes.' There are times he should take out one slip and times he should take out the other. The wise will know when."

LIVING WITH CONTRADICTIONS
Rabbi Naftali Ropshitzer said: "Before my soul was sent down to earth, it was given what seemed a set of contradictory instructions. You must say, it was told, for my sake was the whole world created; you must also say, as Abraham did, I am dust and ashes. My soul was told that nothing in life equals the study of the Torah but that study cannot equal good deeds. It was told to be ambitious but to be satisfied with what it had. And on it went. My soul protested, 'How can one live with such contradictions?' But my protests went unheeded, and my mother gave birth to me. So here I am and here I have been for 40 years, still living with contradictions."

CHAPTER 5

Health and Care
of the Body

Attitudes Toward the Body

Judaism has always attached great significance to the things of the mind. But what is the Judaic attitude toward the body? When we look at the writings of Jewish teachers on the subject, we must come to the conclusion that there is no single attitude. On one hand, some view the human body as God's creation and the means by which the precepts of the Torah are carried out. Therefore, it is extremely valuable and must be cared for and kept healthy, but it is subservient to the mind. On the other hand, there is an idea dating from the Middle Ages that the body is in conflict with the soul: physical appetites interfere with the progress of the spirit to the extent that to lead a life of holiness involves a severe denial of bodily needs. Between these two extremes has emerged a more moderate attitude, in which care for the body is a *spiritual* concern: promotion of the well-being of one's body is a divine command since both mind and body are equally important. This attitude comes very close to the ideal expressed in the Latin tag *mens sana in corpore sano*: "a healthy mind in a healthy body."

As with many other issues, it is not a question of which attitude one should choose: it all depends on circumstances and individual temperament. On one thing all agree—promoting bodily health is essential. It goes without saying that suicide is among the most serious of sins, but it is also strictly forbidden to deliberately cause injury to one's body. The Rabbis quote from Deuteronomy 4:9: "Take utmost care and watch yourselves scrupulously," which they interpret to mean to watch over yourself so that no harm comes to your body. That is why the Sabbath must be profaned in order to save life, and why, when a person is ordered by the doctor to eat on Yom Kippur, it is a sin to fast.

Attending to Bodily Functions

The Talmudic Rabbis say that the verse "You shall not make yourselves detestable" (Leviticus 20:25) implies that the bodily functions—passing water and evacuating the bowels—must be attended to as soon as the need becomes urgent. There is even a special benediction one recites after attending to these bodily functions:

> Blessed is He who has formed man in wisdom and created in him many orifices and many cavities. It is fully known before the throne of Thy glory that if one of them should be improperly opened or one of them closed, it would be impossible to stand before Thee. Blessed art Thou who healest all flesh and doeth wonderfully.

The Rabbis also interpret eating loathsome food, using dirty dishes or silverware, refraining from taking baths, and so forth, as making oneself detestable and to be avoided.

Rabbinic and Medieval Healing

The Talmudic Rabbis and Maimonides, who followed them, are not content to enjoin care for the body in general terms. They give in full detail how health is to be preserved, even to the extent of providing remedies for various ailments. And here lies a problem. There have been so many advances in medicine since medieval times that what the giants of the past considered necessary to promote health is not necessarily so today. Even in the post-Talmudic Geonic period, the Geonim had issued strict orders that no one should resort to cures found in the Talmud unless contemporary physicians approved. Said the Geonim, the Rabbis, authorities in matters of religious law, were not themselves physicians and had relied upon the physicians of their day for medical information. This they shared with their fellow Jews by recording it in the Talmud. Therefore, argued the Geonim, we, too, should seek the medical advice of contemporary doctors instead of using the methods in the Talmud. It follows that in modern times we should heed the opinions of the Rabbis and Maimonides on the promotion of health, but use the methods of modern practitioners of medicine.

Psychological Ailments

Implied in the recognition that new medicinal techniques should be accepted even though they are at variance with older ones is that new methods to heal the mind are as acceptable as those for the body. Psychiatry has helped countless people suffering from mental illnesses. Few Jews are prepared to argue that we should rely solely upon the Torah to heal the mind, not a psychiatrist. While the Torah is balm for the soul, the soul cannot function properly in a sick body, as Maimonides said; neither can it function when the mind is ill. Jewish law, like other legal systems, holds the plea of insanity to be valid when considering responsibility for crime. We cannot fathom why God allows people to be mentally disturbed any more than He allows people to become physically ill. However, since the Torah teaches that God has given permission to doctors to treat the body, there is not the slightest reason for supposing that He has not given them permission to treat the mind as well.

Faith Healing

The question of faith healing is more complicated. Although there is a good deal of charlatanism among some self-proclaimed faith healers, it may be that some people have the power to heal. Most Jews who are sick will consult a doctor trained in scientific methods of healing, but, when all else has failed, they turn in desperation to a faith healer.

Is this permitted? There seems to be no objection among Jewish authorities provided that the healing is not done in the name of another religion, say, Christianity; that, obviously, would not be acceptable. And many would argue that rather than having faith in the healer, one should have faith in God to heal.

Keeping Fit

Taking proper care of our health does not mean it should be an obsession; to be a hypochondriac is itself a sickness. Judaism demands that we have a sensible diet, exercise regularly, and generally try to keep fit without making a fetish of it. Certain habits should be discouraged. For example, it may not be written in any of the sources of Judaism that drug-taking is forbidden, but, since medical opinion as well as common sense leads us to conclude that drugs are harmful to both mind and body, it is surely against the whole spirit of Judaism to indulge in drug-taking or even an occasional "snort."

Alcohol

Judaism, while decrying drunkenness, does not advocate complete abstention from alcoholic beverages. But what constitutes excess? Each individual must be honest in deciding. However, laws against driving after drinking alcohol should be strictly obeyed. In addition to the harm one could cause to oneself, regard for the safety of others must always be in the forefront of one's mind.

Cigarette Smoking

In view of the link between smoking and lung cancer and the probable connection to heart disease as well, a number of Rabbinic voices have been raised, forbidding smoking altogether as a modern extension of the Judaic demand that we avoid taking risks with our health. Yet many Rabbis do smoke cigarettes. Judaism evidently does not forbid us to take risks with our health and safety. If it did, we would not be allowed to cross the road because of the risk that we might get run over. For all that, it certainly is in the spirit of Judaism that packets of cigarettes carry a health warning and that young men and women refuse to become addicted to the weed. Many religious folk feel that whatever the advantages of cigarette smoking might be, they are heavily outweighed by the real disadvantages.

GLEANINGS

MAIMONIDES ON HEALTH
Maimonides was a skillful physician as well as a great Jewish thinker and teacher. In his Code of Law (*Mishneh Torah, Yesodey ha-Torah* 4:1), Maimonides summarizes the traditional Jewish attitude: "Since for the body to be whole and healthy is the way God has ordained—for it is impossible to understand or to know anything about the divine when one is sick—it is necessary to keep away from anything that is destructive to the body, and one is obliged to do that which brings healing to the body."

HILLEL GOES TO BATHE
Hillel, on his way to the bathhouse, told his disciples that he was on the way to perform a religious duty. "Is it a religious duty to bathe?" they asked. "It is," replied Hillel. "If the statues of kings erected in theaters and circuses are regularly scoured and washed by the one appointed to look after them, how much more I, who has been created in the image of God?" [Midrash, Leviticus Rabbah 34:3].

SKILL BETTER THAN PIETY
The question was put to the Lubavitcher Rebbe: Two doctors are available to carry out a certain treatment; one is very skilled at his job but not very religious, while the other is less skillful but deeply religious. Which of the two should be preferred? "Religion has nothing to do with it," the Rebbe replied. "Choose the most skillful."

HYPNOSIS AS A CURE

The famous German Talmudist Rabbi Jacob Ettlinger was the first to discuss whether Jewish teaching permits the use of hypnosis as a cure. Rabbi Ettlinger states that he can see no reason why it should not be permitted since there is nothing magical about the method and, like other natural methods of healing, it is permitted and even advocated by the Torah.

A REBBE IS BETTER

When the Hasidic master Rabbi Simhah Bunem went to Vienna to consult an eye doctor, someone suggested that he try a local faith healer of great renown. Refusing, the Rabbi said: "I am willing to consult a doctor who heals by natural means. But if I am to go to someone who heals by supernatural means, I would rather ask a Hasidic Rebbe to pray on my behalf."

JEWS ARE NOT DRUNKARDS

The well-known Yiddish expression *shikker is a goy* is grossly unfair if taken to mean that only non-Jews get drunk. But it is a salutary warning if taken to mean that it is un-Jewish to overindulge in alcohol.

CHAPTER 6
Life and Death

A Rich Blessing

Judaism emphasizes the importance of life. Our religion urges us to take proper care of our health and stresses that long life is a rich blessing. "I call heaven and earth to witness against you this day, that I have set before thee life and death, the blessing and the curse; therefore choose life, that thou mayest live, thou and thy seed" (Deuteronomy 30:19). "Ye shall therefore keep My statutes, and Mine ordinances, which if a man do, he shall live by them: I am the Lord" (Leviticus 18:5). Yet, sooner or later—we hope later than sooner—everyone now alive will die. Our enjoyment of life is hampered unless we learn to cope with the knowledge that one day our life will end. How does Judaism help us to overcome the fear of death?

Some Jews hold that we must be realistic: death is truly the end, they say, and there is no Hereafter to which we can look forward. According to this view, when our bodies die, we die, so we should face the fact of our ultimate extinction calmly and courageously while getting on with the business of living. While one can admire such stoicism, for most of its existence Judaism has taught that death is not the end. It is hard to believe that the God who made us all created His most precious gift, the human personality, only to eventually destroy it.

There have been many attempts at proving survival through psychic research, for example, but the evidence remains inconclusive. Belief in survival after death is based on religion. If one believes in a benevolent Creator, religious people of many different faiths have said that it follows that He did not endow us with a soul that reaches out to Him only to take it away as if it had never been. To maintain this belief, it is not necessary to explore the geography of Heaven: Maimonides said long ago that we can understand as little about the nature of pure spiritual bliss as a person born blind can grasp the concept of color. We can leave it safely to God; the rest is speculation.

The Jewish view is that we should not look forward to our death since life is good. But, trusting in God, we should not fear death. As Robert Frost wrote:

> The woods are lovely, dark and deep,
> But I have promises to keep,
> And miles to go before I sleep,
> And miles to go before I sleep.

Bioethics

As a result of the tremendous advances in modern medicine, a host of ethical problems concerning vital medical issues have arisen for religious teachers, both Jewish and non-Jewish. As a matter of fact, numerous books and articles have recently appeared on "bioethics"—ethical questions about life and death. In the following pages, the main discussion on Jewish bioethics will be sketched briefly. It must be realized, however, that decisions on these weighty topics cannot be given here; for these we must await the deliberations of the experts, and much is still in flux. Consequently, I shall state the pros and cons of each question so that the reader can see what the various debates are.

Euthanasia

It is possible to keep people alive indefinitely on life-support machines who otherwise would have died but, nevertheless, may never recover. The ethical question is whether it is permitted under Jewish ethics to switch off the machinery prolonging their lives. Would this constitute an act of murder?

Those who argue against switching off life-support equipment hold that the patient is still alive, and to switch off the machines is an act of murder. Furthermore, they argue, to give doctors the right to decide when to terminate human life is to usurp a prerogative that belongs to God; God gives life, and God alone must terminate it.

Those in favor of switching off life-support machinery when there is no hope of recovery and the patient has only a vegetable-like existence argue that such a life cannot be called "life." To disconnect the machinery is not an act of murder since the patient will die as a result of his illness; it only removes an *artificial* method of sustaining life. Furthermore, proponents of this view claim that it is substantiated in the sources of Judaism: the *Shulhan Arukh*, the standard Code of Jewish Law, rules that while it is forbidden to do anything directly that will hasten the death of a dying man, it is permitted, for example, to stop people from making a loud noise in the next room that may prevent him from dying. As for the argument that doctors must not be given powers over life and death, proponents claim doctors already have these powers by practicing their craft and using life-support machines. Some argue that the matter should be decided by the patients' families, not doctors, but others are extremely reluctant to compel the family to make such an agonizing decision. Of course, the laws of the country in which the patient resides need also to be considered.

Praying a Sufferer Dies

A kindred question to the above is whether it is right to pray for the death of a person suffering great agony. Prayers for the sick usually ask that sufferers live, but are there circumstances when it is permitted to pray that terminally ill people obtain a merciful release? The famous fourteenth-century authority Rabbi Nissim of Gerona, known as the *Ran*, contended in his commentary on the Talmud (*Nedarim* 40a) that not only is it permitted to pray for their speedy release, but obligatory. The *Ran* cites a case mentioned in the Talmud (*Ketubot* 104a) concerning the maidservant of Rabbi Judah the Prince, who prayed for his death when she saw that he was in great pain. However, a number of teachers after the *Ran* were uneasy about family members praying for the death of a loved one since—human nature what it is—their unconscious motive might be to seek release from caring for the sick person.

Artificial Insemination

When a husband is incapable of impregnating his wife, they may decide to try artificial insemination—injecting a woman with fertile sperm obtained from a man other than her husband so she can become pregnant. The technical term for this is AID (artificial insemination by donor). Is AID permitted according to Jewish law or does it constitute adultery? The whole question has been fiercely debated by Orthodox authorities, the majority of whom frown upon the procedure. Rabbi Moshe Feinstein has been a lone voice among Jewish authorities supporting AID. Here are the pros and cons.

Arguments in Favor of AID

It is a natural and laudable desire for a woman to want children. Obviously, a married woman would prefer to have children sired by her husband, but if she can only have children through AID and her husband does not object, why should it be forbidden? Adultery occurs only if there is sexual intercourse, not when sperm is inserted into her womb by artificial means. That sexual intercourse without the emission of sperm constitutes adultery shows it is the physical act that counts, not insertion of sperm. Morally, it can hardly be maintained that by undergoing such a purely clinical act solely for the purpose of having a child the wife is being unfaithful to her husband. The child will be at least as much the husband's as one the couple might adopt.

Arguments Against AID

It does not follow that because the act of intercourse without the emission of sperm constitutes adultery that the insertion of sperm without intercourse does not: both may fall under the heading of adultery. But even if no technical or legal adultery were involved in AID, how can it be morally right for a wife to bear the child of a man other than her husband? Such a procedure defies all that is sacred in Jewish married life.

Transplants

The astonishing medical technique of transplanting organs has resulted in prolonging human life and brought hope to sufferers of various diseases. What is the Jewish attitude on this medical issue?

Jewish theologians have never rejected the idea of transplants on the grounds that it is wrong to interfere with nature as structured by God, although other religious thinkers have advanced that argument on similar issues. For example, some Christian theologians in the last century argued against painless methods of childbirth on the grounds that the pain women experience during labor is natural. In the Jewish tradition, it is the glory of humans that they are expected to use their God-given skills to improve upon the unfinished nature that God has created.

Nor is there any objection for a Jew to have a pig's heart as a transplant. The heart is a physical organ, and it is absurd to argue that when a man has such an alien heart his soul or mind becomes tainted.

The main objection to human heart transplants is that a donor may still be alive, which would make the procedure murder. Increasingly, doctors are aware of the problem and take care to see that the "donor" is really dead, although there is discussion on whether lack of brain activity constitutes "death." When the heart is taken from one who has died, the only objection might be that it is forbidden to mutilate a corpse or benefit from one, but these considerations can be set aside in order to save a life.

All we have done with these extremely complicated issues concerning life and death is skim the surface. But it is hoped that the material presented will be some help to the interested reader when pursuing more technical works on these subjects and reflecting on the issues raised.

GLEANINGS

TRUSTING, EVEN IN DEATH
Pious Jews, if they are able to do so, recite the *Adon Olam* hymn just before death. The last stanza reads (in Israel Zangwill's translation):

> I place my soul within His palm
> Before I sleep as when I wake.
> And though my body I forsake,
> Rest in the Lord in fearless calm.

GREATNESS OF HUMAN EFFORTS
The Roman Governor Turnus Rufus asked Rabbi Akiba: "Which is the greater, the work of God or the work of human beings?" To the governor's surprise, Rabbi Akiba replied that the work of human beings is greater. Why? Because God creates wheat, but it is the farmer who plows the field, sows the seed, and reaps the harvest, and it is the baker who makes the flour into dough and bakes bread for people to enjoy [Midrash Tanhuma, *tazria*, 7].

LIFE COMES FIRST
On the question of putting prohibitions to one side when human life is at stake, Samuel quoted the Scripture: *"He shall live by them"* (Leviticus 18:5), but added that "he shall not die because of them" [Talmud, *Yoma* 85b].

CHAPTER 7
Honesty and Integrity

Emet

One of the most interesting words in the Jewish vocabulary is the word *emet* (in the Yiddish form, *emes*). The general translation of this word, "truth," fails to convey its richness. That two and two make four is true, but it is a truth that only has significance when one is counting. In the Bible especially, *emet* denotes personal integrity. The person described in the Bible as "a person of truth" (*ish emet*) is one who is completely reliable, one who does not let others down.

Religious Basis for Honesty

People often say: "Honesty is the best policy," and, indeed, it is. Those who persistently cheat are soon found out and others become suspicious of them, doubting their integrity. The result is that they cannot be successful—even through cheating—since no one trusts them.

But in a sense, the philosophy that honesty is the best policy is merely expedient—that is to say, it is the best policy *for us*. The religious basis for honesty is that it is God's will we be true and faithful and live a life of integrity because God is true and faithful and we are called upon to emulate Him. One should be honest not only because it is the best *policy*, nor for what we can gain from it, but because when we are truthful and honest we are serving God.

Being Honest to Oneself

It is easier to be truthful to others than to be honest with oneself, recognizing one's own faults and acknowledging when one is wrong. One aim of the Torah is to enable us to see ourselves as we are. This does not mean that we must always be looking inward, tormented by guilty feelings. But it does mean that we should make a realistic assessment of our personalities and see life as it really is, not only as we would like it to be. This is part of what is meant when the Torah is called "The Torah of Truth." For example, when we read the stories of Biblical heroes and heroines, we see that the Torah does not hide the faults of even these great men and women. They are not presented as gods or goddesses (Judaism teaches that there are no gods or goddesses) but as people of flesh and blood who make mistakes and cannot attain a life of integrity without struggle. It is something of a pity that, contrary to the whole spirit of the Torah, the great figures of the Bible are often treated as if they have no faults. Such an attitude obscures the truth of the Torah. If Abraham, Isaac, Jacob, Moses, Aaron, and Miriam had to struggle to find the truth, often unsuccessfully, there is hope for us. But if they were paragons of virtue, how can we possibly use the stories told about them to guide our lives?

Cheating

All cheating is a breach of integrity. To cheat in exams, for instance, is utterly wrong not only because we may be discovered, but because it takes unfair advantage of those who work hard to know their subject and misleads those who rely on the results of exams to give us marks and positions. Obviously, a doctor who has obtained certain qualifications through cheating is not really qualified to practice medicine and can do great harm to his patients as well as obtain an unfair advantage over other members of his profession.

It once came to the notice of Rabbi Moshe Feinstein, the famous Halakhic authority, that certain students at a Yeshivah, eager to return to their Talmudic studies, cheated on their exams in secular subjects. When confronted, they argued that their motive was good and asked why they should work hard to obtain the necessary secular qualifications when they felt they could spend the time better studying the Torah. Rabbi Feinstein castigated these students severely, pointing out that a sin with a "good" motive is still a sin. Indeed, it can be far worse than sin with impure motives since the perpetrator justifies it to himself or herself and feels no remorse. The students of the Torah must be especially careful to lead a life of complete integrity, otherwise they are bringing the Torah into disrepute. The same would apply to so-called "religious" people who are dishonest in their business transactions. In addition to wronging their victims, they offend their religion—they are not really religious at all.

Commercial Integrity

Every society has laws governing fair trade, and Jewish law is particularly strict. The Jew is obliged not only to follow Jewish law, but also the laws of the land in which he or she resides. It is possible for an unscrupulous person never to break laws dealing with fair trade, whether Jewish or not, but he or she may still be totally lacking in integrity. Some, for instance, may discover all kinds of legal loopholes so that they are never actually convicted of fraud, yet they make their fortune at the expense of others, which thoroughly defeats the whole purpose of the law. Fair trade depends upon personal integrity. The Rabbis of the Talmud have a special expression for this ideal: going "beyond the letter of the law."

Giving One's Word

Mr. Cohen negotiates with Mr. Levy to buy his house. A price is fixed, to which they both agree, but before the contract is signed, Mr. Levy receives a better offer from Mr. Israels. Mr. Levy then tells Mr. Cohen the sale is off. According to the law, Mr. Levy can do this without suffering any legal penalty since the contract has not been signed. But he had given his word to Mr. Cohen, so it is morally wrong to back out on the deal. As the saying goes: "A man's word should be his bond."

Does this mean that bargaining is forbidden? Certainly not. We are entitled to obtain the best price we can get for whatever we want to sell. But bargaining must take place *before* the deal is made. Once the deal has been concluded to the satisfaction of both sides—even if no actual contract has been signed—it is morally wrong for either party to back out. It would not be wrong for Mr. Levy to tell Mr. Cohen that he received a better offer so that Mr. Cohen might voluntarily up his offer. But Mr. Levy must make it clear that if Mr. Cohen insists upon paying the original price, he will sell it for that. Moral blackmail is not allowed.

According to the Rabbis, Psalm 15 contains a complete summary of how the person of integrity should behave. English writers refer to this Psalm as "the gentleman's Psalm." It is the prescription for life as a Jewish gentleman. (Of course, it is also the prescription for how a Jewish lady should behave.)

> Lord, who shall sojourn in Thy tabernacle?
> Who shall dwell upon Thy holy mountain?
> He that walketh uprightly, and worketh righteousness,
> And speaketh truth in his heart;
> That hath no slander upon his tongue,
> Nor doeth evil to his fellow,
> Nor taketh up a reproach against his neighbor;
> In whose eyes a vile person is despised,
> But he honoreth them that fear the Lord;
> He that sweareth to his own hurt, and changeth not;
> He that putteth not out his money on interest,
> Nor taketh a bribe against the innocent.
> He that doeth these things shall never be moved.

It is worth noting that the Psalmist speaks of his "gentleman" as despising vile persons. To lead a life of integrity is to protest injustice wherever it is found. It is a common mistake to imagine that the religious personality is always calm and never angry. To accept injustice calmly and without despising it is to be indifferent to evil, and no truly religious person can be indifferent to evil. Hatred is usually a harmful and destructive emotion, but not when it is a hatred of evil. To give an obvious example, it is right and proper to hate Hitler. Those who do not are really siding with him against the innocents who were his victims.

Plagiarism

The *Tosefta*, an early Rabbinic work, expands the Biblical command not to steal to include the theft of ideas as well as property. If someone has an original idea or formulates an old one in a fresh manner, he or she owns that idea, and to claim it as one's own is to steal. In the Talmud and subsequent Rabbinic works, scholars frequently reported teachings in the name of the teacher. This is not only for purposes of accuracy—it is important to know the origin of teachings—but also because the originator has a right to be recognized as such.

In modern times there are copyright laws to safeguard ideas presented in books, articles, films, radio, and television, as well as patent laws to protect inventions. But it is ethically wrong to use someone else's ideas without obtaining permission or giving acknowledgment even when the law cannot be enforced. A writer, for example, should not lift ideas or sentences from works written by someone else and palm them off as if they were his or her own. Some writers, unfortunately, just alter another writer's words a little in an attempt to make them their own, but that is still plagiarism. This does not mean, however, that if a writer finds after the fact something he or she has written is similar to someone else's work, it is necessary to acknowledge it. After all, it is not plagiarism if two people hit upon the same idea. Common sense and a healthy conscience are always the best guides on when to provide acknowledgment. (Possibly, more freedom can be allowed speakers when citing every reference will bore the audience.)

Advertising

Advertising is a major industry, and the ethics involved are extremely complicated. Advertising agencies are duty bound to make their clients' goods appear as attractive as possible; they are paid to encourage people to buy. So an element of exaggeration is bound to be present in most advertisements, and would-be customers generally recognize this and take advertising with a grain of salt. It is wrong, however, when an advertisement promises results that the advertised goods cannot produce. A notorious example is to advertise a diet aid that is incapable of helping people lose weight. And if the product contains health-damaging substances, this must be stated in the advertisement, which is why governments rightly insist that packets of cigarettes must contain a health warning.

One practice among some book publishers is to imply reviews of their books are more favorable than they are by taking quotes out of context from reviews. For example, a reviewer may write: "This book could have been a major contribution to the subject if only the author had done his research properly." The publisher may present this in a press release as: "...a major contribution to the subject," which is sure to mislead. The better course is to quote only favorable reviews or not to quote reviews at all.

Advertisers sometimes claim that they are not guilty of misrepresentation when they oversell products since the majority of the buying public has become accustomed to their wiles. There is some truth in this assertion. If some film-makers did not use words like "colossal" or "stupendous" when promoting their movies, customers might conclude that they have no confidence in their works and believe the movies are flops. Admittedly, there are gray areas in this issue. A useful subject for discussion is, When does advertising border on misrepresentation.

Overcharging

A whole chapter of tractate *Bava Metzia* in the Babylonian Talmud deals with the unfair pricing of commodities. The technical term for this is *onaah,* "wronging." The basic rule as formulated in the Talmud and recorded in the Codes is that if the overcharge is less than a sixth of the total value of the goods, it is assumed that the buyer waives any claim he might otherwise have had and cannot demand later that the excess be repaid to him. If the overcharge is exactly a sixth of the total value, the transaction stands but the excess must be returned to the buyer. If the overcharge is more than a sixth, the whole transaction is null and void. In the latter case, the sale is one that cannot be tolerated in Jewish law so *either party* may retract.

Does this mean that the Torah effectively prevents trading for too much profit? Surely people who engage in commercial life wish to get as much out of it as they possibly can. If both parties agree, why should the Torah object? The answer is that the laws of *onaah* are restricted to cases in which goods have a standard market value but the seller has tricked the buyer into paying more while making him believe that he has been given a fair deal. If the goods do not have a standard value, the laws do not apply; the value is what both parties decide it should be. If, for instance, a shopkeeper sells a can of beans with a standard market price of one dollar for two dollars, that would constitute *onaah.* But if a tailor has a reputation for sewing excellent made-to-measure suits, he can charge whatever the customer is prepared to pay for his services. The agreed cost in this situation is the actual value of the suit. Moreover, the laws of *onaah* do not apply to the sale of land even if there is a standard price. The reason? The Talmud was compiled in the agricultural communities of Palestine and Babylon, where land was worth whatever the buyer paid for it since the profits from farming were bound to make the deal worthwhile eventually for the buyer. Nevertheless, some medieval authorities hold in this case that the overcharge must not be more than fifty percent of the total value.

Just as the laws of *onaah* apply to the seller, they apply to the buyer: a buyer is forbidden to trick the seller into letting the goods go for a lower price than they are actually worth.

Judaism does not frown on the profit motive *per se*, but it does object to unfair trading, to obtaining profits through misrepresentation: this is the essential principle by which commercial activity should be governed. A good deal depends, however, upon the individual consciences of those engaged in commerce. People with a healthy conscience will know which transactions involve cheating and which are a legitimate exercise in business acumen. The key text is: "And thou shalt do that which is right and good in the sight of the Lord" (Deuteronomy 6:18).

Misrepresentation

The Talmud contains a number of regulations against misrepresentation in buying and selling in addition to the examples mentioned previously. One may not paint or polish used utensils to make them look new or mix quantities of good fruit with bad and sell the whole without calling the buyer's attention to the bad fruit. The use of false weights and measures is strictly forbidden in Scripture; in Rabbinic times market supervisors were appointed to examine weights and measures to prevent fraud.

In current times similar examples of these types of fraudulent dealings spring readily to mind; for instance, adjusting the mileage gauge of an automobile so it registers fewer miles than the car has actually covered, selling secondhand goods as new, doctoring pieces of furniture to look old and then selling them as antiques, and selling inferior copies of paintings as originals.

This does not mean, however, there is any objection to making goods for sale attractive—using good quality wrappings, for example. There is no misrepresentation here. However, the practice of some supermarkets in arranging less saleable items in convenient, conspicuous areas to tempt buyers may fall within the scope of dishonest trading, but this is matter for discussion.

In professional life, misrepresentation is involved whenever someone claims to have degrees or qualifications he or she does not have. Some "colleges" grant easy degrees for the payment of a fee. To buy one of these is stupid because they are worthless, but misrepresentation is not involved unless it is implied that the degree is from a *bona fide* university. Someone with a doctorate from The College of Worthless Degrees should not have the title Dr. John Doe on his letterhead since it could easily be assumed that his Ph.D. came from a reputable, prestigious school such as Oxford or Harvard.

In the scholarly world, it would be wrong for someone with expertise in one field to pretend to have expertise in another in which he or she has little competence. The reviewer of a book should not take passages out of context with the intent to mislead the readers about the nature of the book. If a reference is given for someone who wishes to obtain a position or entry into college, it is right to call attention to the good qualities of the applicant, but not to lavish praise for qualities he or she does not possess. These are all examples of misrepresentation; what makes it wrong is the harm it may cause others.

GLEANINGS

AN ETYMOLOGICAL NOTE
The Hebrew word *emet* is short for *emenet*, which, like *emunah*, translates as "faith." But faith in this context means "trust." Faith in God, for instance, does not mean simply to believe that God exists, but to trust Him completely since He never abandons His creatures. The same root appears in the word *amen* ("Amen"). When we say Amen, what we are really saying is: "This is true for us and we rely upon it."

KANT
The famous eighteenth-century philosopher Immanuel Kant held that the basis of ethics is what he calls "the categorical imperative." By this he means to do those things you wish all people to do, that which brooks no exceptions. Thus, if all human beings were truthful, they would rely upon one another and truth would be furthered. But if all human beings told lies, none would trust the other and *lying itself would become impossible.*

TRUTH, GOD'S SEAL
The Talmud (*Shabbat* 55a) states: "The seal of the Holy One, blessed be He, is truth." Rashi explains that the word for "truth," *emet,* is formed from the letters *alef, mem, tav*—the first, middle, and final letters of the alphabet. This symbolizes that God is in the present, in the future, and in the past.

ILLUSION AND REALITY
The Kabbalists speak of a world of illusion, a world exactly like ours in every respect except that it is imaginary, not real. A little Hasidic boy, when he heard this, asked his father: "How do we know we are not living in the world of illusion?" The father replied: "If you know that there is a world of illusion, you do not live in one." In another version, the father replies: "We are called to the reading of the Torah and cannot be in the world of illusion, for in that world none are ever called."

THE LAW OF THE LAND IS LAW
Samuel said: "The law of the (non-Jewish) government is law," and, hence, binding upon Jews according to *Jewish* law [Talmud *Gittin* 10b].

YES AND NO
The Talmud states: "Do not mislead others. When you say 'yes,' you must mean 'yes,' and when you say 'no,' you mean 'no.' Do not say 'yes' when, in your heart, you mean 'no' " [*Bava Metzia* 49a].

TRUTH IN THE HEART

R. Safra was reciting the Shema when a man offered him a sum of money for something he wished to buy. R. Safra was willing to sell it, but since he could not interrupt his recital of the Shema, he could not indicate his agreement. The would-be buyer, thinking that the offer was too low, kept on upping it. But R. Safra let him have it at the original price. This, states the Talmud, is an example of "speaking the truth in the heart" [*Makkot* 24a].

CREDIT WHERE CREDIT IS DUE

There are 48 rules a scholar should follow; the final item in the list is reporting a thing in the name of him who said it. "For we know that whoever tells a thing in the name of him who said it brings deliverance into the world, as it is said (Esther 2:22): 'And Esther told the king thereof in the name of Mordecai' " [*Ethics of the Fathers* 6:6].

EVEN IN THE GRAVE

R. Johanan said in the name of R. Simeon b. Yohai: "When a saying is reported in this world in the name of a departed scholar, the lips of that scholar move gently in the grave" [*Yevamot* 97a].

TELLING THE TRUTH

Eastern European Jews used to tell of the man who met his friend at the railway station. "Where are you going?" he asked. "To Lemberg," was the reply. Whereupon the man said: "If you tell me that you are going to Lemberg, you want me to imagine that you are really going to Cracow, and you say that you are going to Lemberg because you do not want me to know that you are going to Lemberg. But I believe that you really are going to Lemberg, so why do you tell me that you are going to Lemberg that I should conclude that you are going to Cracow?"

SELLING ONE'S SHARE IN PARADISE

Some Jewish lawyers discuss a question which may appear to be far-fetched but which was not without relevance.

Suppose a man offers his share in Paradise—the reward he will receive in Heaven after his death—for a price. Is such a sale valid? According to the lawyers, it is not. They argue that if a man is prepared to sell his share in Heavenly bliss, it implies that money in the here and now means more to him. There cannot be much hope for such a person to enjoy Heavenly bliss in the Hereafter, so he really has nothing to sell. The whole transaction is null and void *on the grounds of misrepresentation.*

FALSE PARADE OF KNOWLEDGE
The Talmud says that if a man allows others to conclude that he knows more of the Torah than he really does, he is guilty of misrepresentation.

CHAPTER 8
Offensive and Inoffensive Words

Wronging with Words

According to the Rabbis, *onaah,* "wronging," has two forms: *onaat mamon,* "wronging with money," and *onaat devarim,* "wronging with words." The former has been discussed in the preceding chapter; the latter involves saying something that is hurtful or which can cause harm to others. In most countries there are laws against defamation of character, but according to Jewish teaching *onaat devarim* is forbidden even where the actual laws of slander and libel cannot be invoked. The Rabbis add that a husband must be especially careful not to utter harsh words to his wife since "she is easily moved to tears."

Here are examples of *onaat devarim* mentioned in the Talmud: it is wrong to haggle over something one has no intention of buying since it causes unnecessary distress to the would-be seller. If someone is suffering from a disease or other misfortune, it is wrong to suggest to him that God has caused his calamity because of his sins and that he has only himself to blame. This would apply, for instance, to someone who suffers from ill health because he has been less than careful about his diet. No doubt one should tactfully suggest that he should be more careful in the future, but one should sympathize with him over his plight and avoid adding to his agony by reminding him that it serves him right. It is wrong to taunt a sinner with his former sins. Similarly, it is wrong to remind a convert to Judaism that he or she was not born into the Jewish faith. It is wrong to expose someone's igno-

rance by asking him questions that one knows he cannot
answer. For instance, quoting Hebrew or Latin to someone
who isn't familiar with that language is to "wrong with
words." The Rabbis go so far as to say that it is wrong to
refer to another by a nasty nickname even if he has become
accustomed to people using it; however, the Rabbis only
forbid it when it is intended as an insult.

A further extension of the above principles is to forbid
what the Rabbis call *genevat daat*, literally, "stealing the
mind," allowing others to be misled about one's intentions. In
one example given in the Talmud, A, pretending to be hospi-
table, invites B to be his guest because he knows that B will
be unable to accept for one reason or another. Another example: B is a guest at A's table and A has already opened a
bottle of special wine for his own use. A must not say to B:
"Since you are my guest, I have opened a special bottle of
wine in your honor." On the other hand, *genevat daat* is not
involved if a person jumps to the wrong conclusion. For
instance, while A is taking a stroll, waiting for B to come to
his home, he meets B in the street. B, imagining that A has
come out especially to meet him, says: "How nice of you."
There is no need for A to tell B that he was wrong since B
misled himself.

Putting Others to Shame

The Rabbis are so strict about putting others to shame
that they say: "Whoever causes his neighbor's face to go
white with shame in public has no share in the World to
Come." This is no doubt hyperbole, but it does show the
seriousness of the offense. The Talmud rules that there are
severe penalties for someone who calls another a bastard or
a criminal. The post-Talmudic authorities extend this to one
who says in a quarrel: "*I* am not a bastard or a criminal,"
implying that the other is.

Beyond the Letter of the Law

The following story told in the Talmud has often been quoted in reference to going beyond the letter of the law. Rabbah, son of Huna, hired porters to transport wine from one place to another. The porters were careless, and one of the barrels broke and the wine spilled. When Rabbah took their cloaks as security until they compensated him for the loss, the porters summoned him to the Court of the great Abba Arikha. Abba ordered Rabbah to return the cloaks at once. "Is that the law?" protested Rabbah. "Yes," replied Abba, quoting the verse: "That thou mayest walk in the way of good men" (Proverbs 2:20). So Rabbah returned the cloaks. The porters then argued: "We are poor men and we need our wages." Whereupon Abba said: "Give them their wages." Rabbah again protested: "Is that the law?" "Yes," was the reply since the same verse continues: "And keep the path of the righteous."

The verse Abba quoted refers to going beyond the letter of the law, so how could he have said it was the law? In fact, the law was on Rabbah's side. It is implied in the narrative, however, that the obligation to go beyond the letter of the law *is* the law for a man like Rabbah of whom the highest standards of integrity are expected. The law applies to everyone in all circumstances, while the duty of going beyond the letter of the law depends on circumstances and is not always demanded. But when it is, as with Rabbah, going beyond the letter of the law *is* the law.

Evil Talk

The difference between *onaat devarim* ("wronging with words") and *lashon ha-ra* ("evil talk") is that the former is done to someone's face, while the latter is done behind his back. There are two types of "evil talk": the first is to speak ill of someone, to recount his faults and failings when he is not present to defend himself. The second is usually called *rekhilut* ("talebearing"). This is when I inform B that A has said nasty things about him. Strictly speaking, *lashon ha-ra* and *rekhilut* are two distinct offenses, but both are equally wrong according to Jewish teachings.

A famous Lithuanian scholar, Israel Meir Kagan (1838–1933), observing how much harm was done in Jewish communities by "evil talk," resolved to do something about it. He wrote a book that is now the standard work on the subject, *Hafetz Hayyim,* named for the verses (Psalms 34:13–14): "Who is the man that desires life (*he-hafetz hayyim*) and loves days, that he may see good therein? Keep thy tongue from evil. And thy lips from speaking guile." Rabbi Kagan published his book anonymously, but later his identity was discovered. From then on, Rabbi Kagan became known as the *Hafetz Hayyim.* Many pious Jews use Rabbi Kagan's work as a guide, looking up when it is forbidden to speak ill of others and when it is permitted. (There are occasions when one must speak out in order to avoid a greater wrong.) Some Rabbis considered the somewhat legalistic approach of the *Hafetz Hayyim* to be too tight and precise. One cannot simply look up these matters in a book, they argued; rather, one should be guided by one's own conscience. Of course, the conscience should draw on Jewish teachings and principles, so a proper sense of balance in this delicate area should be preserved.

Rabbi Kagan wrote also a supplementary work entitled *Shemirat ha-Lashon* ("Guarding the Tongue"). In this he elaborates on the principles involved in a less legalistic fashion.

In his works Rabbi Kagan considers the following question: You hear that A is about to go into business with B as his partner, but you know that B has a bad reputation. Or you hear that a young woman is about to become engaged to a young man, but she is unaware that he suffers from a severe illness. If you tell what you know, you will be guilty of *lashon ha-ra,* but if you do not, you will be guilty of a more serious offense: allowing harm to come to someone when you can prevent it. Rabbi Kagan declares that in these and similar instances not only are you allowed to speak out, you are obligated so to do. He quotes the verse "Thou shalt not go up and down as a talebearer among thy people; neither shalt thou stand idly by the blood of thy neighbor" (Leviticus 19:16). Very neatly, he shows the connection between the two parts of the verse: it is wrong to be a talebearer, but, the verse implies, it is a greater wrong to stand idly by and do nothing when the tale you bear can prevent someone coming to harm.

Journalism and Lashon Ha-ra

The question of when to tell and when to remain silent arises in journalism, especially investigative reporting, in which scandals are exposed and wrong done by public figures is described in great detail. Since, as the *Hafetz Hayyim* states, *lashon ha-ra* applies to the written as well as the spoken word, does this mean that journalists are guilty of it? One can argue that by exposing evils in public life, the journalist is doing a public service. That it is his job and he does it in order to win fame and fortune does not render it bad, and, in any event, a good journalist sees his work as valuable to society. It is a moot question whether this applies to gossip sheets, in which tittle-tattle about the famous is cattily written so readers can enjoy feelings of superiority. Hard and fast rules cannot be given: here a person must be guided by his or her conscience.

The Dust of Lashon Ha-ra

The Rabbis have an interesting expression for loose talk that is not exactly "evil talk," but which can easily lead people to think badly of someone: *avak lashon ha-ra* ("the dust of evil talk"). Among the examples the Rabbis give are to say, "There is fire in the house of so-and-so" (implying that they are wealthy and always have something cooking) or to praise someone when people who dislike him are present (they will be tempted to speak ill of him). Telling secrets, apart from breaking confidences, can also result in *lashon ha-ra*.

I Would Say It to His Face

Consider this passage in the Talmud (*Arakhin* 15b–16a): "Rabbah said: 'Anything that is said in the presence of the person who is concerned does not constitute *lashon ha-ra.*' Abbaye objected: 'In that case, it is both impudence and *lashon ha-ra.*' But Rabbah replied: 'I hold with Rabbi Jose who declared that he had never said a word and looked behind his back. Rabbah son of R. Huna said: 'Whatever is said before three (or more) people does not constitute *lashon ha-ra.* Why? Because your friend has a friend, and your friend's friend has a friend.'"

On the basis of this passage, many people do not mind speaking ill of someone when he will eventually know of it, since there is no backbiting. We often say: "If he were here I would say it to his face." The *Hafetz Hayyim*, however, understood the Talmudic passage to refer only to statements that are ambiguous; the fact that it is made to the person's face makes the statement innocent.

Scholarship and Lashon Ha-ra

Often in the Talmud, Rabbis engaged in criticizing one another, speaking ill of their colleagues' opinions, and even hurling abuse at one another. Maimonides' great critic, Abraham Ibn David, does not pull his punches in criticizing Maimonides' rulings. In one instance, he says: "This author is like someone who has no brains in his head." The *Hafetz Hayyim* defends the great teachers' abuse of one another on the grounds that "the Torah burns within them"—in their concern for the truth, they feel obliged to denigrate those they consider to hold false opinions. Even great teachers are, after all, only human and cannot always be restrained from giving vent to their feelings.

In modern scholarship honesty demands that false views should be exposed; that is how scholarship advances. Suppose a researcher believes that a well-known fellow researcher has misled people. He may feel it his duty not only to adduce the evidence but to denigrate the scholar who holds the opposite opinion—otherwise others may follow his colleague as a great authority. Of course, scholars who engage in this kind of personal abuse to enhance their own reputation by destroying that of others are in the wrong; that would constitute *lashon ha-ra.*

In some circles, historians who uncover the faults as well as the virtues of great figures in Jewish history are criticized and their works declared taboo. But there cannot be serious historical investigation unless it is undertaken objectively, so that the truth is allowed to come out. It is useful to know that Jewish heroes had foibles, because that gives "lesser mortals" a degree of confidence that they, too, are not so bad when they fail to live up to high standards.

Harmless Gossip

Most of us enjoy from time to time what we call "harmless gossip." It is *lashon ha-ra,* but we excuse it on the grounds that it is due more to curiosity than to malice. This is a difficult issue: is gossip ever entirely harmless? And yet, while the *Hafetz Hayyim* was able to speak for hours without uttering a breath of scandal, most of us feel that to be sociable we cannot avoid gossiping as well as listening to it. (The *Hafetz Hayyim* says that it is a worse offense to listen to *lashon ha-ra* than to speak it.) At the risk of boring the reader, it is necessary to repeat that ultimately conscience must be the guide. One thing is certain: the malicious motive is always bad. One should never seek to win fame and respect through the denigration of someone else.

GLEANINGS

WORDS CAN HURT

Wronging with words is worse than misrepresentation in commercial activities; with the former, there is no redress. Moreover, it is an offense not only against the neighbor's property but against his person [*Bava Metzia* 58b].

TO EASE MY CONSCIENCE

Rabbi Israel Salanter stated that although it is necessary on the eve of Yom Kippur to beg forgiveness from those we have wronged, if I have said unpleasant things about someone behind his back, I should not tell him and ask him to forgive me. As it is, he remains blissfully unaware, but if I tell him that I have spoken ill of him, it will pain him. I have no right, according to Rabbi Israel, to cause distress to my neighbor in order to ease my conscience. (Other rabbis disagree with him.)

THE LIVING ARE MORE IMPORTANT

There is a ban, said to go back to the Geonim, against speaking ill of the dead or shaming their memory. But the *Hafetz Hayyim* used to say that while most people are reluctant to speak ill of the dead (perhaps for superstitious reasons), they have no reluctance to speak ill of the living or to put the living to shame. The latter, however, is far worse. The dead have gone to their rest and can no longer be hurt by malicious words, but the living can.

THE TONGUE IS GOOD FOOD

Rabban Simeon b. Gamaliel told his servant to buy him good food in the market. The servant brought him tongue. On another occasion he told the servant to buy him bad food, and again the servant brought him tongue. "When the tongue is good, there is nothing better, and when it is bad, there is nothing worse," said the servant. "Death and life are in the power of the tongue" (Proverbs 18:21) [Midrash, Leviticus Rabbah chapter 33].

DON'T BAD-MOUTH YOURSELF

A visitor to Radin, the town in which the *Hafetz Hayyim* resided, asked someone he thought was an ordinary little Jew the way to the home of "the great saint, the *Hafetz Hayyim*." "Oh, you mean Israel Meir," the little man said. "He is no saint. If only you knew him as I do." The visitor was enraged at the insult to the *Hafetz Hayyim* and slapped the man across the face. When the visitor arrived at the *Hafetz Hayyim*'s house, he saw that the man he had assaulted was none other than the *Hafetz Hayyim* himself. Throwing himself at the Rabbi's feet, the man begged forgiveness. The *Hafetz Hayyim* later said that he had learned an important lesson from the episode: it is surely wrong to speak evil of others, but it is also wrong to speak evil about oneself.

TELLING TALES OUT OF SCHOOL
How do we know that one of the judges in a case must not say: "I voted for acquittal, but what could I do since my colleagues, who were in the majority, voted for conviction?" Of such a person, Scripture states: "He that goeth about as a talebearer revealeth secrets" (Proverbs 11:13) [Mishnah, *Sanhedrin* 3:7].

A HELPFUL INSULT
One Rabbi in the Talmud referred to a colleague as "a miserable jackal." Why? The Rabbi felt that his colleague was too ascetic in his behavior and might encourage pious people to follow his example and fail to enjoy life [Hayyim Jair Bacharach].

RISE—AT WHAT COST?
Rabbi Israel Salanter once said to a little boy: "If you want to stand higher than another boy you do not have to push him down. You can leave him where he is, but stand on a chair."

CHAPTER 9
Love Thy Neighbor

Revenge and Bearing a Grudge

Scriptural verse (Leviticus 19:18) says: "Thou shalt not take vengeance nor bear any grudge." The Rabbis in the Talmud (*Yoma* 23a) elaborate on these two prohibitions through examples: A asks B to lend him a sickle (nowadays, it would probably be a lawn mower), but B refuses. The next day B asks A to lend him his axe. If A replies: "You did not lend me your sickle, so I am not going to lend you my axe," that is revenge. If A lends him the axe but says: "I am not like you," thereby demonstrating that he is still sore about B's refusal, he is bearing a grudge.

The Scriptural prohibitions do not apply to property recoverable by law. For instance, if B stole A's sickle, it would not constitute revenge if A summoned him to a Court of Law. Otherwise there would be no means for justice; the Torah does not order us to allow others to take our goods without protest. If B insults A, A is not obliged to take it laying down; he is allowed to hurl insults back at B in defense against further aggression. However, in this instance, the Talmud encourages A to overlook it:

> Concerning those who are insulted but do not insult
> others in revenge, who hear themselves re-
> proached without replying, who perform good
> deeds out of the love of God and rejoice in their suf-
> fering, Scripture says: "But they that love Him be
> as the sun when he goeth forth in his might"
> (Judges 5:31).

Maimonides in his great Code (*Deot* 7:7–8) explains the reason for these two prohibitions—unless people are prepared to overlook their neighbors' lack of good will and to forgive such lapses, society will lose its cohesion. Where there is constant mistrust, commercial life comes to a standstill. Maimonides also observes that "the wise" don't get upset because a neighbor refused to lend them a sickle. Such worldly matters are trivial and not worth getting upset about.

To Love Your Neighbor

Rabbi Akiba said that the verse "Thou shalt love thy neighbor as thyself" (Leviticus 19:18) contains a great principle of the Torah. Everyone knows this verse and agrees with Rabbi Akiba on the great significance Judaism attaches to loving your neighbor. Yet there are very few verses in Scripture that have been so misunderstood. Many sensitive souls have tormented themselves because they think the verse means we are obliged to love others as we love ourselves but, in their honesty, know that they cannot. How can love be commanded? A person can be ordered to do this or that, but love is an emotion and emotions cannot be forced. The very notion of a command in this instance implies that love is a matter of choice, not of feeling.

The True Meaning of the Verse

It is astonishing that this verse is so often quoted out of context. Let us read the entire passage, not simply a part of it: "Thou shalt not take vengeance nor bear any grudge against the children of thy people, *but* thou shalt love thy neighbor as thyself: I am the Lord." In other words, the verse means *act* lovingly toward others by not wishing them harm. If you take revenge or bear a grudge against your neighbor, you are not *acting* in a loving manner toward your neighbor. The verse is not a command to love spuriously. To attempt that is fraudulent. It is impossible to love everyone; obviously there are those whom we dislike, and, since the verse applies to everyone, there are also people we hardly know well enough to love or hate.

Furthermore, Biblical scholars have pointed out that the word *kamokha* from Leviticus, usually translated into English as "as thyself," does not qualify "love" but "thy neighbor." The meaning is not "love your neighbor as thyself," but rather "love him because he is as thyself," i.e., a human being like you, with the same needs, the same hopes, the same right to be treated fairly.

Consequently, the verse can be paraphrased as: "Do not act hateful or vengeful toward others; rather, act lovingly because they are like you and I am the Lord who created both you and them." This does not make the command easy to follow, but at least it can be followed, whereas a command to love others as ourselves is impossible except, perhaps, for the greatest of saints.

Causeless Hatred

Although the appeal "love thy neighbor" refers to how one should act, not how one should feel, Judaism believes that actions have an effect upon the character. The person who sincerely tries to behave decently toward others finds that eventually he or she comes to love them. The sheer effort involved in trying to behave benevolently makes one's character more benevolent. And, while it is not possible to ingrain love for others instantly into one's character, it is possible to control a descent into hatred for others, especially into what the Rabbis call "causeless hatred" (*sinat hinam*). One can avoid the ugly character trait of disliking others for no real reason.

> I do not like thee, Dr. Fell
> But why this is I cannot tell.
> Yet this I know and know full well,
> I do not like thee, Dr. Fell.

Hatred of others, in fact, does harm to oneself as well as to them because feeding on hatred poisons life. We all know those who cannot get on with the business of living, who neglect their own interests because their hatred of others has become an obsession.

Because of the Ways of Peace

Rabbi Israel Salanter is reported to have given the following order of priorities: First, he said, you should care for your own body, your own physical needs. Next, you should care for your neighbor's body, helping him to earn a living and so forth. Then you should care for your own soul. Last of all, you should worry about the state of your neighbor's soul. "Get your priorities right," said Rabbi Israel. "Do not try to improve your friend's character while neglecting to see whether he is adequately clothed and fed." We can see what Rabbi Israel was driving at, but is his order of priorities correct? If so, will it always be correct in every circumstance?

Leviticus refers to "the children of thy people." Does this mean that we must act lovingly only to Jews? By no means. The Talmud states that just as we are obliged to visit the sick, feed the hungry, clothe the naked, bury the dead, and comfort the mourners when those involved are Jews, so, too, must we behave toward non-Jews. The great Rabbinic principle to keep in mind is "because of the ways of peace" (darkhey shalom): promotion of good will and harmonious relationships in society as a whole. In that case, why does the verse speak only of "the children of thy people"? The reason is that the Torah addresses Israelites, not, say, the Egyptians or the Babylonians. But the implications of the verse, especially the ending: "I am the Lord," surely is that when Jews live together with non-Jews, the latter count as "neighbors." A narrower interpretation has been given to the verse, especially during periods of especially strong anti-Semitism. But in Jewish teaching at its best, the wider view of this passage has prevailed. When the Talmudic Rabbis speak of ahavat ha-beriyot, "love of creatures," they mean love of all human beings, each of whom is created in God's image.

Very few Jews limit their philanthropical activities to their fellow Jews. Most are active in good causes whatever the religious beliefs of the beneficiaries. And that is how it should be according to Jewish teaching.

Mysticism holds that all human souls are "sparks" of Adam's soul. Consequently, to love one's neighbor is to love oneself. Is this idea acceptable? If not, is there any way in which it can be made meaningful?

GLEANINGS

REVENGE IS SWEET, BUT . . .

A man is very sensitive to disgrace and suffers keenly when subjected to it. Revenge is sweeter to him than honey; he cannot rest until he has taken it. If, therefore, he has the ability to act contrary to his nature so that he does not hate those who provoke him and removes from his heart all thoughts of retaliation, such a man is truly a hero. It is an attitude that is, no doubt, easy for angels, but is very hard for human beings. Yet this is what the Torah expects [M. H. Luzzatto: *The Path of the Upright*, Chapter 11].

BIBLE DIFFICULTIES

It is not the passages in the Bible that I do not understand that bother me. It is the passages I understand only too well [Abraham Lincoln].

THE TORAH ON ONE LEG

To the would-be convert who asked to be told the whole Torah while he stood on one leg, Hillel said: "That which is hateful unto thee do not do unto thy neighbor. That is the whole of the Torah. The rest is commentary. Go and learn" (*Shabbat* 31a). Rashi, in one version, explains: "The whole of the Torah refers to the ethical side of Judaism, and there is, of course, the religious side as well."

THE REAL CAUSE

A Hasidic Rabbi was asked: "Why do the Rabbis speak of causeless hatred, since no one really hates without cause?" "That is quite true," replied the Rabbi, "but it is often the case that the hatred is not the result of the cause. The cause is often the result of the hatred."

CAUSELESS LOVE
The Temple, say the Rabbis, was destroyed because of causeless hatred. Very well, then, if we are to rebuild the Temple of Jewish life, we should substitute causeless love for causeless hatred [Rabbi Kook].

RESPECT FOR AGE
As a sign of respect, Rabbi Johanan used to rise not only before aged Jews but before aged Arameans (i.e., pagan idolaters) as well. He explained: "Consider how much of life's experience these men have had. Rava would not go so far as to rise before them, but he would give them other tokens of respect" [Kiddushin 33a].

CHAPTER 10

The Inner Life

Religion in the Heart

Philosopher Alfred North Whitehead defined religion as "what a man does with his solitariness." That is certainly not the whole of religion as understood by Judaism, which is profoundly concerned with the obligations one has, both to society and to God. Yet there is still much truth in what Whitehead has said. The religious Jew should have a private relationship with God, an inner life. That is to say, religious exercises should not be a mere parade of piety for the admiration of others but sincere acts of worship, which is possible only if there is a proper sense of religion *in the heart*. The two key words in the Rabbinic literature in this sense are *kavvanah* and *lishmah*.

Kavvanah

Concentration, intention, direction of the mind are various meanings of *kavvanah*. For instance, if one is praying with *kavvanah*, the words of the prayers should not only be uttered with the mouth, but also the meaning should be clear in the mind.

It is not easy to concentrate adequately in acts of worship all or even most of the time. Because of our familiarity with our prayers, there is bound to be a mechanical element to them—like chopping wood with one's mind on other things, as Maimonides puts it. Does this mean that we should only say our prayers at irregular intervals so that they stay fresh

in our minds? No. That cannot be right and proper. If everyone resorted to this, daily prayer and worship would vanish.
We are flesh and blood and our lives are full of distractions.
God does not expect more from us than we are capable of
giving. What we should try to do is see each day as a new
beginning full of challenges. Maimonides advises that first
we should try to have proper *kavvanah* when reciting the
opening chapter of the Shema, and then we can proceed by
stages beyond that in the future.

Lishmah

The word *lishmah* means "for its own sake." For example, "Torah *lishmah*" means to study the Torah not only to
acquire a reputation for learning, but because it is our joy and
duty to understand the rich meaning of the Torah. *Kavvanah*
refers to engaging our mind in what we do. *Lishmah* refers
to motivation, that we do things for the right purpose from the
beginning.

Just as failure to achieve *kavvanah* should not be cause
for despair, the same is true of *lishmah*. The important thing
is to have a full Jewish life even if your motives are not
always the highest.

The Value of Self-Seeking Motivation

A number of Jewish teachers have advised people to
forget about practicing Judaism solely for its own sake. To
have the necessary drive, they claim it is essential to be
motivated by self-interest. Take the following scenario: two
young women resolve to obtain a degree in Jewish studies.
Rachel, deeply religious, studies *lishmah*, that is, she studies
out of her love for Judaism and in her desire to serve God.
Sarah, less religiously motivated, wants to gain recognition
for her scholastic performance and hopes to use her degree
to obtain a lucrative position. She is honest enough to admit
that if the degree offered no prospects of advancement, she
would not try to obtain it, although she has a keen interest in

the subject and enjoys her studies. At first glance, Rachel's attitude is more worthy of admiration, but is it really so superior to Sarah's? Human nature what it is, Sarah will likely do far better at her studies because she is driven by a powerful force: self-interest. Thus, Sarah's attitude is better even from the *religious* point of view.

Peniyot

Particularly in Hasidism, the need for *kavvanah* and *lishmah* was emphasized to such an extent that many of the early Hasidim denigrated famous Rabbis because they believed the Rabbis were motivated by the desire to win fame and fortune, not to serve God. Later Hasidim saw that such an attitude is self-defeating because it suggests that only saintly people are capable of studying the Torah properly, whereas every Jew is expected to study it. Yet Hasidism to this day demands that its adherents avoid *peniyot*. This Hebrew word's root, *panah*, means "to turn aside." *Peniyot* are "turnings aside" from God—in other words, allowing unworthy motivations to enter one's mind. A good deal of Hasidic literature concerning the worship of God deals with the way to avoid *peniyot*.

Doing Wrong with a Good Motive

The Rabbis discuss in the Talmud whether there are circumstances when it is permitted to commit a sin if the motive is good. An example is Robin Hood, who robbed the rich in order to benefit the poor. The Rabbis urge people to be wary about doing wrong for good reasons, although they admit that occasionally an *averah lishmah*, "a sin done with a worthy aim," is at least the equivalent of a *mitzvah she-lo lishmah*, "a good deed performed with an unworthy motive." Yet, since it is easy to fool oneself into believing that one is committing wrong for the glory of God, it is better to avoid entirely doing wrong for a good purpose. Indeed, in some ways such wrongdoing is more blameworthy than wrongdoing for selfish reasons, since one tends to excuse the former, feeling little remorse afterward.

GLEANINGS

LIFELESS PRAYER
"Prayer without *kavvanah* is like a body without a soul" [Bahya Ibn Pakudah].

PURITY AND IMPURITY OF MOTIVE
R. Judah said in the name of Rav: "Let a man study the Torah and keep its precepts even out of impure motivation, for out of impure motivation the pure will eventually emerge" [*Pesahim* 50b].

STUDY TO ACHIEVE GREATNESS
The Rabbi of Munkacs used to tell young students entering his Yeshivah: "Study the Torah in order to win fame as a great scholar, and this will give you the driving force to become one. It is time to think about studying *lishmah* when you *are* a great scholar."

EARTHBOUND PRAYERS
The Baal Shem Tov once stood at the door of a synagogue and said that he could not enter because it was crowded. "But the place is empty," exclaimed his disciples. "No, it is full of all the prayers that have been recited without proper concentration and intention," he replied. "Only prayers recited in the love and fear of God are capable of rising to Heaven."

THE REGULATED LIFE
The Vilna Gaon said that once the Torah has been given, there is no longer room for sins to be committed *lishmah*. Otherwise, why bother with the detailed laws of the Torah? All we would need to do would be to look at our motive and, if it were good, do whatever we wanted. Once the Torah has been given, right is right and wrong is wrong whatever the motivation.

CHAPTER 11
Good Deeds

Good Deeds

Maasim tovim, "good deeds," refers to acts of charity, kindness, and benevolence. The Talmudic Rabbis speak of "Torah and good deeds," by which they mean the study of the Torah coupled with acts of benevolence. If study of the Torah leaves the character unmoved and heartless, it is not counted as the true study of the Torah. This is the meaning of the Rabbinic saying "If one declares: 'I shall have nothing but Torah study,' such a person does not even have Torah study to his credit."

Tzedakah

The word tzedakah in the Bible means "righteousness"—that is, behaving justly and fairly, doing the right thing. It is revealing that in the post-Biblical tradition of Judaism the term has come to mean "charity," "almsgiving," and "helping the poor and needy." One can interpret this evolution of meaning as a warning not to feel superior to the poor you help financially. They are doing as much for you in receiving your aid as you are doing for them by giving it. They are entitled to be helped by their more fortunate brethren. When you give to them, it is tzedakah—doing the right thing—not an extraordinary act of piety. God gave you the wealth you have, and you are a steward of God. What you distribute to the needy ultimately belongs not to you but to Him.

The Laws of Tzedakah

In the Jewish tradition, there are detailed rules and regulations for *tzedakah* regarding the right manner in which charity should be collected and distributed. The *Shulhan Arukh* has a whole section devoted to these laws. However, they are not meant to be enforceable; they are largely appeals to individuals to behave as Judaism would have them behave. Nevertheless, in many Jewish communities penalties have been imposed upon rich people who sought to evade their duty to contribute to charity funds. Every Jewish community worthy of the name has a society for poor relief. In Talmudic times, the town's poor were to be given food, shelter, and clothing. Poor folk visiting the town had to be provided with a bed for the night and with two square meals each day and three on the Sabbath.

Some Rules and Regulations

According to the rules in the standard codes, every person is obliged to give *tzedakah*, even the poor. For them, a very small amount is equivalent to massive contributions of the wealthy. However, a poor man should not give away money or food that he needs to support his family.

Many pious Jews follow the Biblical custom of tithing by giving a tenth of their profits each year to charity. This custom originally applied only to agricultural proceeds, but the Rabbis extended it to cover all business profits. This is known as *maaser kesafim*, "the tithe of money." Some authorities say that tithing is not an actual obligation, but "a custom of the worthy." Some pious folk go so far as to give a fifth of their profits to *tzedakah*. But, the Talmud states, no one should give away more than a fifth because that might result in impoverishment and becoming a burden upon the community.

It is wrong for one to help poor people who are no relation rather than help the poor members of one's own family. Similarly, it is wrong to support the charitable enterprises of other towns while neglecting those of one's own. The order of precedence is one's own poor relations, the other poor of the town, then the poor of other towns. Of course, one must have a sense of proportion and not follow too blindly the rule of precedence. Jews have a reputation for responding readily to calls for help, whether they come from near relatives or strangers, from Jews or non-Jews.

The highest form of *tzedakah* is to help a man in financial distress from becoming poor. For example, one could loan him money to tide him over or give him employment.

One should not give to the poor with a glum face or do anything to cause them embarrassment. Put yourself in the other's place, urge the Rabbis. Imagine how you would feel if you had to be supported by charity. Give cheerfully, offering kind and encouraging words. It is better not to give at all than to insult the poor by implying, for instance, that they are destitute because they are work shy.

It is notorious that the worthy people who collect and administer funds for charity regularly receive insults, both from the wealthy, from whom they collect, and from the poor, who complain that they are not receiving their due. That is why the Rabbis say that charity collectors and administrators are "greater" than those who merely give.

Nowadays, there are trained professionals engaged in charitable work. For them, it is a full-time occupation for which they receive a salary. What Judaism demands of them is that they have a proper sense of vocation: they should be caring people who have respect for the ones they are called upon to help.

It is praiseworthy for a poor man to avoid taking charity if he can avoid it—by taking a job, for instance, for which he might otherwise feel unsuitable. But if a poor person is really in need, he or she is obliged to take from the charity funds. There is no merit in a person who needs help but is too proud to take it.

Gemilut Hasadim

This lovely expression means literally "bestowing kind-nesses." It is different from *tzedakah*; the latter applies only to giving of one's wealth, whereas *gemilut hasadim* applies to every act of kindness, from giving someone a helping hand to saying a few words of cheer to someone who is sad or worried. Other examples include visiting the sick, attending weddings and funerals, comforting mourners, even telling jokes if this will cheer up a friend or promote friendship. In fact, as the name implies, *gemilut hasadim* has more to do with inner character than with outward acts through which character expresses itself. In other words, there cannot be any regulations for the practice of *gemilut hasadim* as there are for *tzedakah*. The ideal is for a person to have a loving and caring character so that kind acts or words follow of their own accord.

GLEANINGS

THE TORAH PERSONALITY

If someone studies the Torah but is dishonest in business and discourteous to others, what do people say about him? "Woe unto him who studied the Torah, woe unto his father who taught him Torah, woe unto his teacher who taught him Torah. This man studied the Torah—see how ugly are his ways." But if someone studies the Torah and is honest in business and speaks pleasantly to others, what do people say about him? "Happy the father who taught him the Torah, happy the teacher who taught him the Torah, woe to those who do not study the Torah, for this man who studied the Torah see how fine his ways, how righteous his deeds" [*Yoma* 86a].

THREE KINDS OF NUTS

Rabbi Levi said: "There are three kinds of nuts—those with soft shells, those with middling shells, and those with very hard shells. The first kind can be opened easily. The second kind open if you knock them. The third kind are hard to break, and even if you do manage to open them, they do you no good. The same applies to the Jewish people. Some give charity without being asked. Others are like the middling nuts— when they are asked to give, they give at once. Others, even if you press them to give many times, it does no good."

GIVING 'TIL IT HURTS
During the early nineteenth century, a time of great poverty and distress in the Russian community, the renowned Hasidic leader Rabbi Shneour Zalman of Liady wrote to his followers, asking that they disregard the Talmudic rule against giving more than a fifth. "For," he argued, "such a rule does not apply when the poor are in dire need and starving."

SENSITIVITY IN GIVING
The Talmud tells of a wealthy man who would leave money at the door of a poor man's house without telling him so the man would never know the identity of his benefactor. Another wealthy man would place a sum of money in a bag over his shoulder so that the poor could take the money without him knowing their identity. But, the teachers add, best of all is to give charity so that one does not know the identity of those poor who have benefitted and the poor do not know the identity of their benefactor. How can this be achieved? Give quietly to the charity overseer and beg him not to say a word about it when distributing to the poor.

DEATH THROUGH PRIDE
Jews in Eastern Europe tell of a poor man who preferred to starve rather than apply for poor relief. As a result, the man died. People said of him that he did not die of starvation; he died of pride.

CHAPTER 12
Work and Leisure

Is There an Obligation to Work?

In the King James Version of the Bible, the Fourth Commandment reads, "Six days shalt thou labor, and do all thy work. But the seventh is the sabbath of the Lord thy God; in it thou shalt not do any work" (Exodus 20:9–10). Does this mean that there are two separate commandments: 1) Do not work on the sabbath; 2) Do work on the six days of the week? If this is the meaning of the verse, Judaism demands that we must work during the week—when we work, we are carrying out a religious duty, we are performing a *mitzvah*.

A Rabbinic panegyric on the high value of work (*Avot de-Rabbi Natan*, version 2, chapter 21) reads: "Just as Israel is *commanded* to keep the sabbath, Israel is *commanded* to work" (italics mine). This suggests that there is a command to work. The Protestants interpret the verse in this manner, but what is the Jewish understanding?

It may be that the Fourth Commandment's six-day workweek is supplementary to the command to keep the sabbath; that is, do whatever work is necessary for sustenance during the six days of the week and refrain from it on the sabbath. The *New English Bible* interprets the verse similarly: "You have six days to labor and do all your work. But the seventh day is a sabbath of the Lord your God; that day you shall not do any work." The syntax of the original Hebrew bears out this interpretation.

It is going beyond the evidence, however, to infer from the verse that idleness is an offense against the Ten Commandments—although the Fourth Commandment does imply that part of the divine plan is for man to work. Too much idleness is frowned upon by Jewish moralists, but occasionally, it has value as an antidote to irksome business. Judaism does not take issue with the poem by William Henry Davies:

> What is this life
> If, full of care,
> We have no time
> To stand and stare?

Judaism sees work as a means to an end, not an end in itself. If it were and working were a *mitzvah*, the workaholic should be admired for zealously trying to get in as many *mitzvot* as he can during each day. High value, however, is placed on work in the Jewish ethic. Human dignity is enhanced when a person, in the language of the Psalmist, "eats the labor of his hands."

The Talmudic Rabbis engaged in a number of occupations ("work" was not necessarily construed by them to mean manual labor) in order to earn a living. According to the Talmud, a father is obliged to teach his son a trade or craft so he can earn an honest living. The Talmud (*Kiddushin* 118a) also gives advice concerning the occupations one should not follow because they are degrading or disrupt the character.

The human spirit is discontent unless one earns one's keep, say the Rabbis (*Pesahim* 118a). They base this observation on the Biblical verse, "Cursed is the ground for thy sake; in toil shalt thou eat of it all the days of thy life. Thorns and thistles shall it bring forth to thee; and thou shalt eat the herb of the field. In the sweat of thy face shalt thou eat bread" (Genesis 3:17–19). The rabbis imagine Adam was terribly disturbed when he heard that he was to eat the herb of the field, for this would have made him no different from his ass whose food was ready at hand. But when he heard that he was to toil for his daily bread, Adam's mind was set at rest. "In the sweat of thy face shalt thou eat bread" is seen not as a curse, but rather as a reassurance to people that their dignity will not be compromised in their incessant search for sustenance. To work in order to earn a living is to be independent.

But Is Total Independence Possible?

Of course, no one is truly independent. We all depend upon God for our very lives and "no man is an island," as John Donne has said. Human beings are social beings: on the whole, the work we do is possible only in society, and a just society seeks to provide suitable conditions of employment.

Human beings work, consequently, not only to earn a living. Part of the motive to work should include the desire to make a contribution, however small, to society and posterity. (Judaism can hardly accept H. G. Wells' very facile protest: "What has posterity done for me that I should work for posterity?") As The Midrash puts it:

> The Holy One, blessed be He, said to Israel: "Even if you find the land full of all good things, do not say that we shall sit back and refrain from planting, but take care to plant shoots. Just as you found when you entered the land trees planted by others so you, too, must plant on behalf of your children."

The Therapeutic Value of Work

We have noted two reasons why working is admirable from the Jewish point of view: one can earn a living while acquiring a degree of independence; and it fulfills an obligation to the future of the human race. But a third reason is found in the Jewish sources: the therapeutic value of work. According to the old proverb, "All work and no play makes Jack a dull boy." But the Rabbis reverse the proverb when they remark: "Idleness leads to dullness."

The Rabbinic panegyric on work contains this saying: "If a man has no work to do, let him find some. If he has a run-down yard or field, let him go and occupy himself with them." These days, the equivalent could be to do odd jobs about the house, help with the wash, take up carpentry, or do gardening. It is interesting that bodily activity is advocated. Possibly, the Rabbis were thinking of people for whom intellectual pursuits had no attraction, or, more plausibly, in the absence of sports during Rabbinic times, some physical effort was advised even for the scholar.

The Use of Leisure

It would seem from reading Rabbinic literature that the only worthy pursuit outside working is the study of the Torah. The Rabbis had no hobbies and evidently saw little need for relaxation, unless the picture we have of Rabbinic life in ancient times is overly idealized.

While the problem of leisure time may not have loomed very large for the ancient Rabbis, it does for contemporary society as machines increasingly free people from the need to spend long hours of the day in backbreaking toil. For this reason, the Jewish work ethic needs to be extended to embrace leisure.

We live in a very different world from that of our ancient teachers, a world in which new questions, unimagined by them, are being asked. They did not experience capitalism or organized labor; they did not have mass unemployment, recessions, or complex economic problems on a global scale; there were no travel agents and package holidays, no science and technology, no retirement and superannuation. We can only hope to discover indirect guidance from the past and need to work out the rest for ourselves.

But this does not mean that Judaism leaves us without principles. It is a counsel of despair to believe Judaism has no bearing upon modern-day problems and situations. There is, after all, a Jewish work ethic, in which it is taught that human beings are ennobled by work; that human beings, created in God's image, are entitled to their dignity and need to be spared from searing humiliation; that they are required to use both work and leisure for something higher and better than mere survival; and that, since each individual is unique, a just society that still manages to preserve individual liberty is doing God's will. These are the principles, and they are as applicable today as they were in ancient times. The rest, as

Hillel said in another context, is commentary. But it is a commentary still to be written.

Trust in God

Although it is a general principle in Judaism to trust to God to provide, one still needs to make an effort to take care of oneself. The Rabbis have been insistent in pointing out that one must not rely upon miracles and that God helps those who help themselves. Yet trust in God is still required when human effort is made.

Torah and Derekh Eretz

Derekh Eretz means literally "The Way of the Land." The expression denotes ethics in general, good conduct, and proper behavior. But derekh eretz can also mean engaging in business or following a trade. It is used in this manner when Rabban Gamaliel III wrote in Ethics of the Fathers (2:2):

It is good for the study of the Torah to be combined with some worldly occupation (derekh eretz), for the effort demanded by both of them makes sin to be forgotten (i.e., one is too busy to have time to sin). All study of the Torah without work must in the end be futile and become the cause of sin.

Samson Raphael Hirsch, the great nineteenth-century German Orthodox leader, extended Rabban Gamaliel's saying in a novel way. Western culture, said Hirsch, is our derekh eretz; it is a means of enriching personality. Hence Hirsch's slogan "Torah and Derekh Eretz" means that it is not only permitted but desirable for a Jew to be cultured and well educated as well as to be a student of the Torah. Great literature, painting, and music are, for Hirsch and his school, extremely worthy pursuits in their own right.

In recent years, however, there has been opposition to Hirsch's philosophy by some traditionalists. They have argued that Jews are obliged to devote as much time as possible to study of the Torah. While these traditionalists do not object to studying other subjects to earn a living, they believe general subjects should only be studied as a means to an end, unlike the Torah, which should be studied for its own sake. The Hirsch school retorts that the values of Western culture equip people for richer intellectual and even spiritual lives and, thus, are good in and of themselves.

A Well-Rounded Life

No one who is aware of the joys of Jewish learning and the tremendous application required to become proficient in the Torah will have anything but admiration for those who devote themselves exclusively to Torah studies. Yet there is a degree of one-sidedness, which Hirsch saw, in the total rejection of Western cultural value. To most of us, it would doubtlessly seem extremely narrow-minded to refuse to enjoy good music, great art, and literature. We want Mozart and Beethoven as well as Synagogue music, Rembrandt and Michelangelo as well as paintings of the shtetl, Shakespeare and Dickens as well as the Talmud, Kant and Spinoza as well as Maimonides. Of course, once one becomes more open, certain challenges are presented to Jewish belief and discrimination is required. Yet Hirsch and his followers rightly argue that traditional Judaism is capable of meeting the new challenges as it so successfully met the old.

Relaxation

It would be dishonest to pretend that we never indulge in reading for pleasure as well as for edification. We read thrillers and other novels, watch programs on television that are not always serious or informative, and perhaps enjoy pop music and farces at the theater. A sense of balance and propriety should be maintained, however. It is impossible to lay down rules to cover all these situations, so individuals must be guided by what they consider to be suitable according to the values of Judaism. Life is not always serious, and there should be room for relaxation, humor, and a dose of sheer frivolity. The important thing is to avoid the meretricious, the vulgar, the obscene, and the spiritually harmful. The Talmudic Rabbis, for instance, objected to Jews watching gladiatorial combats, because participants routinely died, and to their attending the Roman theater, because Judaism was mocked there. Most people are sufficiently discriminating to appreciate the difference between watching, say, a Marx Brothers' film and a striptease.

GLEANINGS

A BENEDICTION FOR WORK?
If it is a *mitzvah* to work, why is there no special benediction to be performed before carrying out one's daily work, as there is a benediction before carrying out other *mitzvot*?

WORK IS NOT DEGRADING
The great Babylonian teacher Rav told Rav Kahana, his disciple: "Rather skin a carcass in the marketplace for a fee than be supported by charity. Do not say: 'I am a priest,' or 'I am a scholar,' and that it is beneath your dignity" [*Pesahim* 113a].

SUPPORT OF FAMILY
"Happy are they that keep justice, that do righteousness (*tzedakah*) at all times" (Psalm 106:3). Who is the one who does righteousness all the time? It is the person who works to support the family [*Ketubot* 50a].

FOR POSTERITY
A Rabbi saw an old man planting trees. "Why do you plant trees," he asked the man, "since you will never enjoy the fruit?"

The old man replied: "I found trees planted by my ancestors from which I enjoyed the fruit. Surely, it is my duty to plant trees for those who come after me to enjoy" [*Taanit* 23a].

A PRAYER FOR SUSTENANCE

O God, Who providest food and raiment to every creature, open Thy loving hand unto me and sustain and give me nourishment in a useful and honorable calling. Help me to support my household by lawful and not forbidden means and in a manner free from all shame, disgrace, or dependence on mortals. Let me walk in the way of the upright before Thee and deserve the blessing of prosperity upon my undertakings. May I be enabled to assist all sacred causes and be privileged to extend help and hospitality to others who are in need. Shield my home from all evil; let peace and well-being abide in it; and in me may the Scripture be fulfilled. *Thou openest thine hand and satisfiest every living thing with favor.* Amen [The Hertz Prayer Book, p. 236].

IS WESTERN CULTURE BANKRUPT?

Some rabbis have argued recently that Western culture is bankrupt, demonstrated by the fact that one of the most cultured European nations produced Hitler, the Nazis, and the World War II death camps.

CHAPTER 13
Gambling and Taking Risks

Gambling

In discussing Jewish attitudes toward gambling, a distinction must be made between the legal and ethical aspects. The questions that need to be asked are whether Jewish law forbids gambling and whether gambling is ethically sound. The second question depends upon the answer to the first: if Jewish law forbids gambling, then it must be morally wrong to gamble. If, on the other hand, Jewish law does not forbid it, the second question arises, since it does not follow that because a certain course is legal that it is ethically desirable.

The Legal Attitude

According to the Talmud (Sanhedrin 24b), there are two possible reasons for forbidding gambling. The first is because the gambler earns his living in a nonproductive manner, making no useful contribution to society. The other reason is more subtle: unlike any other business contract, the loser's agreement to pay the winner is not given wholeheartedly. He only bets because he hopes to win. When, for example, A buys goods from B, he agrees to the sale without reservations although it may ultimately prove unprofitable. But when A plays poker, he only agrees to allow B to pocket the winnings if B wins because A believes that *he* will win or, at least, A hopes he will. When A loses, he pays his debt, but he does so with a strong degree of reservation. It can be argued, consequently, that when B pockets the winnings, he is really taking that which does not legally belong to him, making it theft. Although one authority in the Talmud views gambling in this way, the other opinion is more commonly accepted. For B to pocket the winnings is legally correct since, after all, A knows the risk he is taking when he makes a bet and agrees to play the game of his own free will.

The Difference between These Views

We have two possible reasons to forbid gambling according to Jewish law: 1) The gambler makes no useful contribution to society, and 2) The gambler is not entitled to pocket his winnings because they are not given freely. The second reason, however, is not recognized by most Talmudic authorities. Consequently, only the first reason stands, and this would only apply to an habitual gambler, one who has no other occupation. The notion among some non-Jewish moralists that gambling is wrong because the winner gets something for nothing is not found in Jewish sources. Judaism holds that it is not wrong *per se* to get something for nothing, any more than it is wrong for someone to profit, say, from the oil he has found beneath his land.

Having a "Mild Flutter"

There is no *legal* objection to people having "a mild flutter"—backing horses, playing cards for money, buying a lottery ticket, or betting on the outcome of a boxing or football match. In Eastern Europe, groups of devout Jews organized lotteries, giving the proceeds to good causes.

The Moral Question

The basic objection to gambling in any form is that it can so easily become addictive. Everyone knows the misery caused to the family of a man addicted to gambling and the misery he himself feels. Once a person become addicted, he is ready to risk everything, his wealth, his job, his happiness, to satisfy his craving. It is then that gambling becomes a real vice. Ultimately, it depends on whether a person is sufficiently strong-willed to stop before gambling endangers his well-being and hurts others. Anyone who senses that it can become an addiction is well advised to not have even the mildest of flutters.

The Goral

The casting of lots (goral) is, in a way, a form of gambling, but it is mentioned in a number of instances in the Bible (Leviticus 16:8–10; Numbers 26:55; Joshua 15; Samuel 14:42–43; Jonah 1:7; Esther 3:7). A question that arose in the Middle Ages was whether it is permitted to use the Bible as a goral, that is, to open the Bible at random and then be guided by the verse that appears on the open pages. Although the great teacher Maimonides strongly opposed magical practices (he considered them to be nonsense), he appeared to be tolerant about Bibliomancy—provided it was seen only as an "indication," not as an actual oracle (Mishneh Torah, Avodah Zarah 11:5; Responsa, No. 173). A number of recent works refer to a form of Bibliomancy known as Goral ha-Gra (The Goral of the Vilna Gaon) in which the Bible is opened at random and paged through by sevens until an appropriate verse appears. (For some reason this is attributed to the Vilna Gaon, although there is no evidence for the correctness of this attribution.)

Taking Risks

Gambling is one thing, taking calculated risks is another. If people always play it safe in life, they rarely achieve great things. The operative word here, however, is "calculated." When young men and women decide which course of studies to pursue for a career, they have no guarantee that they are choosing the right one or that they will be successful. But if they honestly believe that they have chosen well, they take the risk and place their trust in God.

Gazing into the Future

There is a fine line between consulting the Bible and using the kind of divination the Bible condemns to decide which course of action to take. For the good Jew, palmistry, fortunetelling, and the like should not be taken seriously. It is far better to do whatever one can to secure one's future and leave the rest to God. That is the course recommended by Rashi on the basis of the Biblical passage "Thou shalt be perfect with the Lord thy God" (Deuteronomy 18:13). This verse comes after ones forbidding divination and magic. According to Rashi, the verse means "walk before God wholeheartedly, put your hope in Him, and do not attempt to investigate the future, but whatever it may be that comes upon thee accept it wholeheartedly, and then thou shalt be with Him and become His portion." In other words, it is not only the use of magical means to determine the future that is wrong but the use of legitimate means as well; the person who trusts in God will leave the future safely to Him.

Mazzal Tov

The congratulatory *mazzal tov* had its origin in astrological beliefs, beliefs that the destiny of human beings was determined by the stars. *Mazzal tov* means "a good star." In the Middle Ages, Maimonides rejected astrological beliefs on the grounds that to believe that anything other than God could determine human fate was to compromise monotheism. Nevertheless, we use the expression, and it is, of course, no more than a harmless way of wishing others good luck or congratulating them on their successes. It only becomes contrary to the Jewish spirit when people really believe that luck is an entity that can be petitioned as in a song from *Guys and Dolls*: "Luck Be a Lady Tonight."

GLEANINGS

GIVING WHEN WINNING

Although the Talmud states that one should not give away more than a fifth of one's wealth, many Jewish teachers say that this only applies to capital for which one has worked hard. One who wins a large sum of money in a lottery should give thanks to God by donating some of the winnings to charity. Here it is desirable to give very generously, even if it amounts to more than a fifth of the winnings.

ADDICTION TO GAMBLING

The seventeenth-century Venetian rabbi Leon de Modena wrote a treatise on the evils of gambling when he was 14. He must have known even at that early age where the shoe pinched, for in later life he described the miseries that resulted from the passion he developed for the vice he had so eloquently condemned in his youth.

COMING UP WITH THE RIGHT ANSWER

It is rumored that Rabbi Aaron Kotler could not make up his mind whether to accept the advice of his friend Rabbi Moshe Feinstein to settle in the USA or whether he should live in Israel. He performed, it is said, the *Goral ha-Gra* and came up with the verse: "And the Lord said to *Aaron*: 'Go into the wilderness to meet *Moshe*'" (Exodus 4:27).

SOME HUMAN EFFORT REQUIRED

A man kept praying to God: "Please let me win the forthcoming lottery." A friend overhearing the prayer asked: "How can you hope to win if you have not bought a ticket?"

CHAPTER 14
Hard and Soft Virtues

The Virtuous Character

While Judaism is deeply concerned with deeds, it is also concerned with the character that inspires good deeds. There are many references in Jewish sources both to *maasim tovim* ("good deeds") and to *middot tovot* ("good qualities" or "virtues").

In Judaic philosophy, virtues are divided into hard and soft. Among the hard virtues are courage, strength of character, steadfastness, and self-control. These are "hard" because they require their possessors to have the ability to say "no" to others and especially to themselves. People with these qualities have to be men and women as hard as iron.

The soft virtues include compassion, gentleness, flexibility, love, and sensitivity. These are "soft" because their possessors must have a degree of pliability in their character. They have to be, to a certain degree, "softies."

The trouble is that the two sets of virtues are in contradiction. The harsh character may find it easy to be courageous and steadfast but difficult to be compassionate. Conversely, the soft character can be kindly and generous without difficulty, but finds it hard to be stern and unyielding when these qualities are required. Since the ideal Jewish character requires soft qualities at times and hard ones at others, each individual has a struggle on his or her hands.

Individual Temperament

People naturally differ in character and temperament. Some are volatile, but have a sweet disposition. Others are lethargic, with a sour temperament. The art of Jewish living is to use whatever disposition one has. One must be sufficiently honest with oneself to recognize the flaws in one's character and try to overcome them, while encouraging the strengths. But there are limits to the degree character can be changed. Wisdom consists of self-acceptance; doing the best with what we have; avoiding too much introspection; getting on with the business of living; and thanking God for creating a rich variety of creatures, no two of whom are exactly alike in temperament any more than they are in bodily form.

There comes a time when a bad-tempered person, try as he must to keep his anger under control, ultimately has to live with it and see the futility of wishing for a serene disposition, just as an ugly man who wants to be physically attractive does.

Courage and Steadfastness

The tension between the hard and soft virtues is most evident in obedience to the truth. On one hand, if truth is to be the guide, it must be fought for courageously. On the other, there is the danger that people with strong convictions may become what the Israelis call "principle-nudniks," bores who ride rough shod over the opinions of others, always insisting that they alone know what is best. One needs to be both firm when truth demands it and yielding whenever possible without compromising the truth. That such an attitude is difficult no one will deny.

Unless Jews had been determined to hold fast to their faith no matter how hard the road, Judaism, as the religion of a minority group, would not have survived. Many Jews throughout the ages have been prepared to sacrifice their lives rather than be disloyal to the truth. This is the positive side of the expression "a stiff-necked people," used in Scripture pejoratively to describe the stubbornness of the children of Israel. In the personal life of a Jew, great courage and steadfastness are required to lead a proper life despite temptation. The old saying "It is hard to be a Jew" is very true. There is joy in Jewish living, but, like anything else worthwhile, a price has to be paid. Discomfort, even agony, has seemed to many faithful Jews a price worth paying for their religion.

And yet the iron in the Jewish soul must be tempered with gentleness. Even when one is in the right, one should not view those in the wrong as motivated by disdain for the truth. Yes, there are many occasions when it is essential to do battle for the right, but there are other times when the sword should be allowed to rest in its scabbard.

Pious and learned Jews are often tempted to look down upon those less pious and learned. In a way, a degree of pride in Jewish learning is unavoidable, and it may even be desirable, if it is not overdone. The Rabbis put it quaintly when they say that a *talmid hakham*, a scholar in Torah learning, is allowed to have "an eighth of an eighth of pride," although one Rabbi has protested that since pride is an abomination, one should not have even the slightest degree of it. The most distinguished Rabbis and Jewish saints always knew how to be compassionate to others, even to sinners. As one of the great Jewish preachers put it: "The bush burns with fire, but the bush is not consumed." *Nor does it consume others.*

Hard on Oneself, Easy on Others

Rabbis are often called upon to render decisions on difficult religious questions if there are problems arriving at the correct solution. That is why they often differ on the correct ruling in some circumstances. As their guide in doubtful cases, many famous Rabbis have adopted the principle "Be strict for yourself but lenient for others." Of course, if the law clearly forbids a certain action, a Rabbi is required to state the law. But if there is considerable doubt about what the law actually is, these Rabbis have tried whenever possible to use a permissive ruling for others (perhaps by relying on earlier permissive authorities), but have always applied a stricter ruling to themselves.

Ways of Pleasantness

Jews have an obligation to present the Torah way of life as an attractive one, but this does not mean that they must water down the religion, especially if they wish to retain their loyalty and integrity. But it does mean that they should dwell more upon the delights of Jewish living rather than present Judaism as a burden to be carried purely out of a sense of duty. Their tone should be conciliatory, not severe, and they should only resort to rebuking another if it is absolutely necessary. One Rabbi in the Talmud went so far as to say that he doubted whether anyone in his generation was fit to rebuke others. Few things are more off-putting than fanaticism, even in pursuit of a good cause. This is why some Jews are fond of quoting the verse "Her ways are ways of pleasantness, and all her paths are peace" (Proverbs 3:17). In the original context, the verse refers to wisdom in general, but since Rabbinic times it has been applied to the Torah. The verse is sung in synagogues all over the world when the Scroll of the Torah is returned to the Ark after the reading. It has been understood to mean that the way of Torah not only *is* pleasant but should also be *seen* as pleasant.

This applies to ethics as well. In the name of "goodness," some people are anything but good, condemning the failures of lesser mortals who generally retaliate by calling good stupid. In Elizabeth Wordsworth's lines:

> If all the good people were clever,
> And all clever people were good,
> The world would be nicer than ever
> We thought that it possibly could.
> But somehow, 'tis seldom or never
> The two hit it off as they should;
> The good are so harsh to the clever,
> The clever so rude to the good.

Being a "good" Jew includes being "clever"—clever in the sense of being wise and understanding. The ways of Torah wisdom, after all, are ways of pleasantness.

Sentimentality and Toughness

Some people, in their laudable desire to see Judaism presented in an attractive and captivating manner, mistakenly adopt a sentimental approach to Jewish life, making it seem schmaltzy. This can become far more off-putting than an over rigorous approach. Men and women of good taste and sense appreciate that Judaism makes severe demands on its adherents. And this applies to non-Orthodox trends as well as Orthodox. A religion that makes no heavy demands upon its adherents is not a real religion. God is described as "Father," but a loving father (or mother) makes demands on his children and does not indulge them. As C. S. Lewis puts it, some people do not want a Father in Heaven but a Grandfather in Heaven, a senile deity who, at the end of the day, can remark that a good time was had by one and all.

An element of toughness should be present in the ideal Jewish character, including the ability to say no, not only yes. While it is right and proper, for instance, to depict the joys of the shtetl and to sing joyful Hasidic songs, it is a distortion of the truth to overlook the darker side of shtetl life, its misery, poverty, and obscurantism. Hasidic joy, rightly understood, is joy in the service of God, a stage that in its higher reaches only the saintly can attain. Thus, Hasidic melodies and dance are byproducts, rather than the real thing.

Life is a serious business, and Jewish life, for all its joys, is more serious than most. Salo Baron is right to scorn what he calls "the lachrymose picture" of the Jewish past, but it has not always been tragic. There have been periods—such as the Golden Age in Spain—when Jews were affluent, highly cultured, and able to enjoy life in all its richness and produce great works of permanent significance. But how can anyone today overlook the tragedies in Jewish history, the Holocaust, the pogroms, the death camps? And what sensitive person can remain indifferent to human suffering the world over—the wars, the wholesale destruction, the starvation of children in a world in which food is plentiful? We can obtain only glimpses of why God created a world in which there is so much evil. But, Judaism teaches, He wants us to fight evil, and this means that we are being both superficial and irreligious if we go through life singing "God's in His Heaven, all's right with the world." It is this line of thought that is behind the Talmudic saying that it is forbidden for the mouth to be filled with joy in this world. Only in the Messianic Age, when war and hatred have been totally vanquished, is the fullest joy realizable. Only *then*, in the language of the Psalmist (Psalm 126:2), will "our mouth be filled with laughter and our tongues with singing." Sentimentalism is no substitute for a realistic appraisal of the human situation.

Worry and Anxiety

Taking life seriously does not mean that its humorous side should be ignored or that one should constantly chew the past over and be anxious about what the future might bring. A degree of worry is not without value, but to worry too much about the outcome when we have done our best—or to be obsessed with problems we cannot possibly solve—is doubting divine providence. After all, the religious person believes God is in control of His universe.

This is why the Hasidim believe that too much anxiety betokens lack of faith and why the true Hasid is joyous. The Hasidim tell of a man who came to the Kotzker Rebbe for help because he was always worrying about his future. "Why not pray to God for help?" asked the Kotzker. "I cannot pray," the man replied. "In that case," declared the Kotzker, "you really have something to worry about."

GLEANINGS

BEING SOFT, BEING HARSH
The kindly person is in danger of being too soft with himself just as he is soft on others. The pious person is in danger of being harsh because he is hard on himself. The intelligent person is in danger of losing his faith because he tends to question everything. Does that mean that a Jew must not strive to be kindly, pious, or intelligent? Certainly not. He must strive to be all three, and then the personality will achieve poise and balance.

THE QUALITIES OF THE PATRIARCHS
Each of the patriarchs, according to the Kabbalah, had his own special quality. Abraham was especially magnanimous. Isaac was especially rigorous. Jacob was balanced between the two extremes. There are times in Jewish life when one must call upon the quality of Abraham, other times upon the quality of Isaac, and still others upon the quality of Jacob.

STRENGTH AND GENTLENESS
Judah ben Tema said: "Be bold as a leopard and light as an eagle and swift as a gazelle and strong as a lion to do the will of your father in Heaven" [Ethics of the Fathers 5:20].

ALWAYS BE PLIANT
Rabbi Simeon ben Eleazar once came from the home of his teacher elated that he had acquired so much learning. While in this frame of mind, he saw an ugly man and asked him: "Are all the men of your town as ugly as you are?" The man replied: "Go ask God why He made me so ugly." Rabbi Simeon, realizing his fault, bowed before the man, begging him for forgiveness. At first the man refused to forgive him, but when he was entreated to do so by the people, he pardoned Rabbi Simeon on the condition that he would never repeat that mistake. Thereupon Rabbi Simeon entered the House of Study and preached: "A man should always be soft as a reed and not hard as a cedar tree. It is because of its softness that the reed is privileged to be used for the making

of pens with which Torah scrolls, *tefillin,* and *mezuzot* are written" [*Taanit* 20a–b].

TWO MEDIEVAL SAYINGS ON WORRY
The only thing to worry about is worrying itself.

> The past is in store.
> The future's before.
> God's help's at the door.
> Worry no more.

CHAPTER 15
Sexuality

Talking About Sex

Not so long ago it would have been impossible to include a chapter on sex in a book on ethical attitudes intended for a general readership. Nowadays, when hardly any teenager is ignorant of "the facts of life" and discussions on sexual topics are dealt with daily in the media, it would be absurd to avoid the subject. In fact, Judaism has never encouraged excessively prudish attitudes toward sex. The Talmudic Rabbis frown upon *nivul peh* ("dirty talk"), but that is a far cry from a frank consideration of what Judaism has to say about sexuality.

A rabbi writing on this subject faces the difficulty of how to state the high standards demanded by Judaism without appearing to be insensitive to the real problems that people— especially the young—have with sex. What a rabbi must do, nevertheless, is describe the Jewish attitude to the best of his ability without softening its rigors. Difficult though it is, there are still many thousands of young people who live up to these high standards and are prepared to swim against the current of present-day sexual mores.

The Sex Instinct

The majority of Jewish teachers hold that the sex instinct, created by God, cannot be unworthy. Maimonides alone follows Aristotle in saying that "the sense of touch is shameful," but even this great teacher realized that sex is an important part of human life that cannot be thwarted. When the Talmudic Rabbis speak of the *yetzer ha-ra,* "the evil inclination," they are usually thinking of the sex instinct, but they only call it "evil" because it is so powerful. Uncontrolled, it can easily lead a person into evil. In a well-known Midrash, there is a comment on the words "very good" found in the creation narrative at the beginning of the book of Genesis. When the Torah says "good," remarks the Midrash, it refers to the *yetzer tov,* "the good inclination." But when it says "very good," it refers to the *yetzer ha-ra.* Without this inclination, no one would marry and life would lack its driving power.

Because they were conscious of the strength of the sexual drive, the Rabbis were honest enough to admit that they were not immune from sexual temptation, although they refused to yield to it. That is why there are so many injunctions in Jewish religious literature on the need for self-control in this area. The Rabbis' general prescription is to avoid dwelling on sexual matters and to marry early in life. The latter was obviously a counsel of perfection in many Jewish communities of the past—and it certainly is today, too, because of economic conditions, for one thing. Another piece of advice from the Rabbis is to study the Torah. When the mind is engrossed in study, lustful thoughts are banished, or so it was held. Everywhere in the Torah, the ideal presented is to attempt to obtain purity in thought and deed.

Sex in Marriage

According to the Jewish tradition, for a husband and wife to have marital relations is a *mitzvah,* "a religious duty." The primary purpose of marriage is to have children. Some of the Jewish mystics hold that the sex act, even within marriage, should not be pleasurable, but carried out as any other *mitzvot,* purely as a religious obligation. But apart from this minority view—and it was intended only for mystical adepts—Jewish teachers see sex as the most intimate expression of love between a husband and wife, a good in and of itself quite apart from the *mitzvah* to propagate.

There is even a discussion concerning why a benediction is not recited before the enjoyment of sex as there are benedictions for other physical enjoyments. Of course, it is obvious that a benediction cannot be recited when the body is uncovered, and those who discuss the question know this. What they are trying to convey is that legitimate sexual pleasure is a divine gift for which God is to be thanked, in the mind at least, if not by speech. Moreover, Judaism does not share the Victorian view that only men should enjoy sex while women endure it passively. On the contrary, a husband is duty bound, according to the Rabbis, to satisfy his wife. He is not allowed, for instance, to be away from home on business for long periods without the wife's consent, and if he refuses to have sex with his wife, it is grounds for divorce.

Contraception

On the use of artificial methods of contraception within marriage, there are differing opinions among the Rabbinic authorities, so Jews should consult their own rabbi. But there is a definite tendency toward leniency, especially concerning the use of birth-control pills.

Extramarital Sex

Judaism demands complete faithfulness in marriage; adultery is strictly forbidden in the Bible. All erotic behavior, such as flirting, hugging, and kissing between a wife and a man other than her husband or between a husband and a woman other than his wife is equally forbidden. (An innocent peck on the cheek in greeting is another matter, although the majority of Orthodox rabbis frown upon even this.)

Celibacy

Although the Talmud and the *Shulhan Arukh* suggest that one who is "in love with the Torah" may postpone marriage or even be celibate all his life, this is hardly ever acted upon. Scholars are enjoined to marry so their studies can be done "in purity," that is, they will be able to study without being tormented by sexual thoughts.

Premarital Sex

In recent years, people have had greater caution when engaging in premarital sex because of the fear of AIDS. But that is not the religious reason for abstaining from premarital sex. It is a sorry comment on contemporary attitudes that it is no longer considered shameful for people to "live in sin." However, one or two Rabbinic authorities rely on the Biblical institution of the "concubine" to permit a man and woman to live together as husband and wife without being married. But even this minority view permits extramarital sex only if the couple are completely faithful to one another and are not promiscuous. If that is the case, they might as well be married *ke-dat Moshe ve-Yisrael*.

Masturbation

In the Rabbinic tradition, masturbation is forbidden. The Rabbis refer to this as "wasting of seed" (although this does not mean that sex within marriage is only permitted if the wife can become pregnant; no one has ever suggested that sex is forbidden if the wife is beyond the age when she can conceive). Yet the frequent references in Judaic literature to the need to atone for "sins of youth" when one marries seem to suggest that masturbation is not uncommon, if not excusable. Because of the emphasis on "waste of seed"—which obviously does not apply to women—female masturbation is hardly ever mentioned as an offense.

Homosexuality

In modern times, the argument has been put forward that some people have a "natural" disposition toward homosexuality, which they can as little help having as, say, a red-haired man can help his hair color. In fact, in the Jewish sources there are no references to homosexuality as a condition. What the Torah strictly forbids is the sex act between two males. In English this is frequently called "sodomy," on the basis of Genesis 19:5, where the men of Sodom wished to abuse the two men who had arrived at Lot's house. But this term is not used in the Jewish tradition for male homosexual acts; instead, the term used is *mishkav zakhar*, "lying with a male." This is because for the Rabbis the main sin of Sodom was that of injustice and cruelty rather than sexual offenses.

Homosexuals sometimes claim that their disposition is not an illness but an alternative lifestylc. In the Jewish tradition, male homosexual practices are termed an "abomination." In our tolerant age, it is considered wrong to punish consenting adults for engaging in male homosexual practices, and it is for God and their own conscience to determine whether they are motivated by emotions over which they have no control. But it is hard to see how Judaism can condone what the Torah considers to be an abomination.

Lesbianism, female homosexual practices, is also not condoned, but it is dealt with far less severely than male practices, probably because there is no penetration.

Interdating

Judaism has always looked upon marrying outside the faith as betrayal. If many Jews took this step, Judaism would soon vanish. But in our society, young men and women constantly meet people of the opposite sex who are not Jewish and yet to whom they are attracted. The only reliable course for those who wish to be loyal to their religion is to limit dating to Jews. To argue, as some do, "I shall never marry outside the faith, and I trust myself not to fall in love," is to court disaster. When one has fallen in love, it is usually too late.

A Summary

Judaism does not consider sex to be unworthy or "shameful." Sex should be seen as a divine gift for the enrichment of life. But the highest standards are demanded for exercise of the sex instinct. That it is always hard to live up to these standards cannot be denied. Yet faithful Jews try to keep these standards and, in the process, further the ideal of the Jewish people as "a kingdom of priests and a holy nation."

GLEANINGS

RESISTING TEMPTATION

Some women who had been rescued from bandits were lodged in the upper story in the house of Rabbi Amram the Saint, and the ladder, by which the upper story was reached, had been removed. Rabbi Amram, seeing through the sky-light how beautiful one of the women was, seized the ladder, which ten men could not raise, set it up, and began to ascend. Halfway up, though, he cried out: "A fire is burning at Rabbi Amram's house." When the scholars came to help put out the supposed fire and saw what had happened, they said: "We have put you to shame." But Rabbi Amram replied: "Better that you shame Amram in this world than that you be ashamed of him in the next." The yetzer ha-ra came from him then in the shape of a column of fire, and he said to it: "See, you are fire and I am flesh, yet I got the better of you" [Kiddushin 81a].

A SENSE OF PROPORTION

In "The Holy Letter," the famous teacher Nahmanides puts forward the view that sex within marriage is sacred. A number of contemporary Rabbis have urged that marital relations should ideally take place twice a week, unless both the husband and wife agree to a less frequent physical relationship. The Rabbis claim it is a mistake in piety to avoid sex except to produce children.

A CONCUBINE

Maimonides in his Code holds that only a king was permitted to have a concubine. Otherwise, why has there been the emphasis in Jewish tradition on marriage under the huppah with the proper marriage service "according to the law of Moses and Israel," *ke-dat Moshe ve-Yisrael?*

THE SIN OF SODOM

"Behold, this was the iniquity of thy sister Sodom: pride, fullness of bread, and careless ease was in her and in her daughters; neither did she strengthen the hand of the poor and needy" [Ezekiel 16:49].

THE MARRIAGE IS NULL AND VOID

Rabbi Moshe Feinstein rules (*Iggerot Moshe*, Vol. 7, No. 113) that if a wife discovers that her husband regularly commits homosexual acts, the marriage can be dissolved without a *get* on the grounds of misrepresentation. Had she known of his proclivities, she would never have consented to the marriage, and it is therefore null and void.

INTERMARRIAGE AND MARTYRDOM

The English Jewish minister the Rev. Morris Joseph reminded young people in a sermon against intermarriage that if they had lived in times of religious persecution, they might have been prepared to give their lives for their religion. Nowadays a less severe, though still very difficult form of martyrdom is demanded of those who would be faithful to Judaism. There may come a time when young Jews and Jewesses have to surrender their tenderest feelings in order to be true to themselves and their religion.

CHAPTER 16

Family and Friends

The Family

In the Bible there are numerous references to the family as the unit around which the life of the community revolves. In the tenth chapter of the book of Genesis, the "families" of mankind are listed, all members of the larger family descended from Noah. Small wonder, then, that Jews have always been interested in family relationships: "You know A. Well, he married B and she is C's cousin, related, by marriage, to D." In recent years, many Jews have conducted determined searches for their "roots," part of the individual's quest for his or her Jewish identity.

Size of Family

According to Jewish tradition, it is a positive command (*mitzvah*) to "be fruitful and multiply." That is, to marry and have children. However, a debate sprang up between the Houses of Hillel and Shammai two thousand years ago concerning the *mitzvah* of establishing a family according to the Halakhah. The House of Shammai said that the minimum number of children is two sons. The House of Hillel also held that the minimum is two, but they specified a son and a daughter. (Many commentators understand this to mean a son and a daughter *or* two sons.) Of course, not everyone is blessed with children, so that, unlike other *mitzvot*, it does not depend entirely upon a person. This is why prayers for children have been so much a part of the Jewish tradition.

Although two children were the number debated by the two houses, larger families were considered a blessing. Nowadays, it has become fashionable even among Orthodox Jews to have smaller families, but the motivation should not be selfish.

Bringing up Children

No parent will agree that it is easy to raise children. There are constant worries about the children's health, education, care, and behavior when they are little and about their career and marriage prospects when they grow up. Jewish parents probably worry too much about their children. Wisdom requires that children must be allowed to develop their own personalities, even at the price of allowing them to make mistakes. Even making these allowances, rearing children is difficult. An old Jewish expression for this is *tzaar giddul banim* ("the pain of bringing up children"). The verse in Genesis (3:16) usually translated as "in pain shalt thou bring *forth* children" is interpreted by the sixteenth-century scholar Obadiah Sforno as "in pain shalt thou bring *up* children." Animals, too, suffer when giving birth, but only humans have the anxieties associated with raising children.

Few Jewish parents are unwilling to pay the price, though, for children are a joy. The great Jewish hope is to enjoy "nachas" from offspring. And to enjoy "nachas" from grandchildren is an even greater delight, especially when children and grandchildren follow in the Jewish ways. The Shotzer Rebbe commented on the old division of all things into minerals, plants, animals, and humans: minerals have no offspring, but they do not suffer decay. Plants do have offspring, but only when the parent plant has decayed. Animals have offspring during their own lifetime, but they cannot recognize the offspring of their own offspring. To human beings alone is given the precious gift—in the language of our prayers—of "children and children's children engaged in the study of the Torah and the practice of the *mitzvot*."

The Family: Cooperation

The family has been described, no doubt unfairly, as a conspiracy—unfairly because a healthy family goes about its work most of the time without thinking in terms of "us" (family members) versus "them" (everyone else). Yet in a sense, the family naturally gives preference to its own members because they cooperate with each other in furthering their own happiness and well-being. In this sense the family is like an individual. While the life of an individual is inadequate if one does not reach out to others, one's own needs should not be left to others to satisfy. By the same token, the ideal family should be outward-looking, but that should not result in neglect of its own members.

Nepotism is unfair and should be avoided. But to invert nepotism, passing over one's own to favor strangers, is equally unfair. If A has to decide whether a position should be given to B, his nephew, or to C, a complete stranger, he should decide which of the two would best fit the position to be fair. If B is the more suitable, it would be wrong to give the position to C merely because it would look like favoritism to give it to B. And in a family business, it might be better to favor B even if C is the best-qualified candidate for the job.

Family Tensions

Everybody knows that even in the best adjusted families tensions arise among the members. Parents usually imagine that they know what is good for their children, while the children often claim to know not only what is best for them, but what is best for their parents. And there is, of course, sibling rivalry. Give and take is essential in family relationships, particularly when some members of the family imagine that other members are in danger of "letting down the side."

Wise parents will try not to show that they are fonder of one of their children than the others. Wise children should not seek to curry special favor with their parents and should avoid talebearing. Parents generally can make each of their children feel that he or she is special. However, if a parent cannot help being especially fond of their youngest or oldest child, say, they should make it clear that any extra love they seem to bear for that child is due simply to an accident of birth, not because of any special qualities the child possesses.

Ethical Wills

Throughout the ages, parents have given advice to their children in their last will and testament. Israel Abrahams has published a collection of such instructions under the title, *Jewish Ethical Wills*. But advice is one thing: for a parent to seek to govern the lives of his or her children from beyond the grave is quite another. Leaving instructions for one's children to do something they do not wish to is a form of moral blackmail.

Adoption

Jewish law does not address legal adoption, but in the Aggadic literature great merit is attached to one who brings up an orphaned child as his or her own.

In most countries these days, there is legal adoption. The question often arises whether those who adopt infants should tell the children later that they are adopted or whether they should be left to assume that they are the natural children of their adopted parents. It should be done very tactfully, of course, but the wisest course is to inform the child at a suitable time that he or she is adopted, otherwise there is always the chance the child may find out on his or her own. If a couple has children of their own in addition to adopted children, great care should be taken not to discriminate between the natural and adopted children. The same applies to stepchildren.

If There Is Conflict Between Parents

If a husband and wife have strong disagreements, the children should avoid taking sides, even if they feel that one parent is in the right. Even more importantly, the children should keep out of their parents' quarrels if their mother and father are divorced. It is also wrong for a divorced parent to try to influence the children in his or her favor. The Fifth Commandment: "Honor thy father and thy mother," still applies even though the parents are no longer husband and wife.

Maimonides and other codifiers rule that the Fifth Commandment applies even if the parent is a criminal or a notorious sinner. Children should never sit in judgment on their parents. According to Jewish law, children are not allowed to testify against their parents when the latter face criminal charges. Parents, too, are barred from testifying in a Jewish Court of Law against their children.

Obeying Parents

Parents should not behave in a dictatorial fashion, issuing orders to their children which they must obey without question. Indeed, it is far from certain that the Fifth Commandment means that there is an obligation for children to *obey* their parents, which is not necessarily the same as to respect and honor them. The famous fifteenth-century authority Rabbi Joseph Colon, known as *Maharik*, discussed a question based on this issue (Responsa *Maharik*, No. 167), which became the basis for all the subsequent debates. The *Maharik* had been asked if a son needs to give up a young woman he loves and wishes to marry if his father orders it. The *Maharik* ruled that on a matter that affects the son's future happiness, the father has no right to make demands, so there is no obligation for the son to obey his father in this matter. The *Maharik*'s ruling is recorded in the *Shulhan Arukh* (Isserles in *Yoreh Deah* 240:25).

Of course from the ethical point of view, children are not always right in defying their parents' wishes, just as parents are often entitled to try to influence their children. A good deal of mutual respect and consideration is required, and each case should be approached with caution. If strong emotions are involved, both parents and children should seek reconciliation rather than strife. The rules and regulations concerning the Fifth Commandment are laid down in the *Shulhan Arukh*, but ultimately it is the "fifth *Shulhan Arukh*" of sheer common sense that should be followed.

In Matters of Torah

Although the Talmud generally frowns on children disagreeing with the opinions of their parents, much depends upon the nature of the disagreement. In matters of Torah, it is not only permitted but obligatory for each individual to pursue the truth as he or she sees it. The Rabbi of Munkacs, R. Hayyim Eleazar Shapira (Responsa, *Minhat Eleazar*, Vol. IV, No. 6) lists famous Torah authorities who disagreed with their fathers and teachers.

Friends

In addition to our families, most of us have close friends with whom we have stronger relationships than some family members. Families as a whole often have friendly relationships with several other families. Far from opposition to this in Judaism, friendship is held to be of value. In a famous passage in the second chapter of *Ethics of the Fathers*, Rabban Johanan ben Zakkai asks his disciples to find the best and worst thing in pursuit of the good way. Rabbi Joshua replies (2:9) that the best thing is to have a good friend, the worst to have a bad friend. An earlier teacher in *Ethics of the Fathers* (1:6) urges: "Get yourself a teacher and acquire a friend." In the Bible there are the narratives which speak of the great friendship between David and Jonathan and between Ruth and Naomi.

Family and Friends

Loyalty to friends is sometimes in conflict with family loyalties, as shown in the story of David and Jonathan. Jonathan incurred the severe displeasure of his father, King Saul, because the king saw David as a threat to his throne. However, the example of Jonathan need not be emulated when there is a conflict of loyalties. The individual must choose according to circumstances.

Friendships Good and Questionable

There are no objections for Jews to have non-Jewish friends, provided that they agree to differ in matters of religion. The Talmud tells of the close friendship between Rabbi Judah the Prince and a Roman Emperor. Even in the Middle Ages, when the conflict between Judaism and Christianity was fierce, some Rabbis had Christian friends. In modern times, it has not been unknown for Orthodox rabbis to be friendly with Reform rabbis. Indeed, a cynic might say it often seems that an Orthodox rabbi can get along better with a Reform rabbi than with some of his Orthodox colleagues. There is nothing surprising in this. Friendship with someone different in outlook poses less of a threat than friendship with someone who has similar opinions and beliefs. This is why greater enmity is often found among supporters of the same political party than among political opponents.

It is doubtful whether it is advisable for a husband to have a strong friendship with a woman other than his wife or for a wife to have this kind of relationship with a man other than her husband. The usual plea in such circumstances is that it is only a platonic friendship and quite innocent. Are such friendships ever completely innocent, though? And even if they are, what of the hurt and embarrassment that may be caused to the spouse? On the other hand, a husband should not be offended if his wife occasionally prefers the company of her female friends, and a wife should not be offended if her husband joins a men's club and has an occasional "night out with the boys."

GLEANINGS

LETTERS IN THE SCROLL

The Jewish mystics say that each letter in the Sefer Torah represents a Jewish soul. Since each letter is important, the Sefer Torah cannot be read if even a single letter is missing. But a letter has no meaning on its own; there are no single-letter words in Hebrew as there are in English, such as the word "a." Words, however, formed from individual letters represent the family. The verse, formed from words, represents the particular Jewish community to which the individual family belongs. The chapter represents the Jewish community as a whole. In turn, the Jewish community belongs to the world community, represented by the Sefer Torah.

YIDDISH SAYING

Small children, small worries; big children, big worries.

GOD'S NACHAS

An old lady once said to God: "Dear God. How can I bless you? If with wealth, you have all the wealth in the world. If with wisdom, you have all the wisdom. So I bless you: May you have nachas from your children."

FAVORITISM

Resh Lakish said in the name of R. Eleazar b. Azariah: "A man must not make a distinction among his children, for on account of the coat of many colors which our ancestor Jacob made for Joseph, Joseph's brothers hated him" [Midrash, Genesis Rabbah 84:8].

A FAMILY CONFERENCE

Rabbi Joseph Laib Bloch, the Rabbi and Rosh Yeshivah of Telz in Lithuania, would call a conference whenever an important family matter had to be considered and allowed every member of the family, even the youngest children, to share in the deliberations.

ADOPTED CHILDREN
Pharoah's daughter brought up Moses as her own child. This tells us that whenever someone brings up an orphan boy or girl in his or her home, Scripture considers the child the person's own [*Megillah* 13a].

WHO TO OBEY?
A question discussed by the Codifiers is what a child should do when his divorced parents give him or her contradictory instructions. The general rule is that the child has freedom of choice regarding whom to obey. One case used as an example by the nineteenth-century teacher Rabbi Akiba Eger (Responsa, No. 68) concerns a father and mother who left their offspring contradictory instructions in their wills.

RELIGIOUS DEFIANCE OF PARENTS
In the early days of the Hasidic movement, many parents ordered their sons not to join. The Hasidic leaders followed the *Maharik*'s ruling that in a matter of such significance, the Fifth Commandment does not apply, and encouraged the young men to join the movement.

STUPID PIETY
Rabbi Yosef Hayyim, the great Baghdadi authority, discussed the case of a pious son who used to sign his name A, son of B, with the writing sloping upward so the father's name appeared higher than his (*Torah Lishmah*, No. 269). Is there any advantage in this? No, according to Rabbi Yosef Hayyim. This is an example of "stupid piety" (*hasidut shel shtut*).

FRIENDSHIP
When we add to the example of David and Jonathan the deep friendship of two women, Ruth and Naomi, we realize that the Bible is also the supreme Book of Friendship [Rabbi J. H. Hertz].

A LIFE WITHOUT FRIENDS
A saint who fell asleep for 70 years found when he awoke that all his friends had died. So he, too, asked God to let him

die. Rava quoted in this connection the popular proverb "Either friendship or death" [*Taanit* 23a].

CHAPTER 17

Humans and Animals

Animals

Our concern here is not with the question of why God created animal life—on this there is a wealth of material—but with the ethics of the human-animal relationship. Nevertheless, it might be appropriate to say something first of the theological aspects.

We have some idea of why God created human beings since they have a moral sense. But what is the purpose of creating animals? So far as one can tell, animals do not have freedom of choice. They can do neither good nor evil, and their destiny is mapped out by their very nature. Consequently, it is difficult to understand why animals exist.

Are Animals Here for Humans?

There are two views among the medieval Jewish thinkers. One is that animals and all other things were created for use by human beings. Animals provide people with food and clothing. They can by kept as pets, promoting caring and compassion in people. The richness of the animal creation— the innumerable species of fish in the sea, for instance—helps to sustain the sense of wonder in human beings and turn their thoughts to God as the Creator of this richness.

The other view, adopted by Maimonides, is that it is pointless to ask why God created animals, as it is pointless to ask why God created anything at all. We can only say that it is the will of God and accept it in wonder. In this view, man may be the highest creature in God's universe, but he must not imagine that God has no other purpose than to provide for human fulfillment.

Treatment of Animals

One thing is certain, whether or not animals were created for the benefit of human beings or whether they fulfill some other purpose, human beings must care for animals and it is forbidden to cause them unnecessary pain. The Rabbinic term is *tzaar baaley hayyim*, "causing pain to animals." And yet Judaism permits killing of animals for food (although according to many Jewish teachers, *shehitah* performed in the proper manner is calculated to reduce the pain to a minimum). Consequently, the operative word is *unnecessary*. Of course, such a term is relative. When is pain caused to animals *necessary* and thus permitted, and when does it overstep the boundary to become forbidden? Various attempts have been made to provide answers for this question. For instance, Rabbi Ezekiel Landau of Prague in the eighteenth century stated that he felt it is forbidden to hunt animals for sport both because of the unnecessary pain it causes the animals and because it wastes the resources of the planet. He remained unresponsive to the hunter's plea that pain to the animal is necessary for the hunter to obtain the pleasure of the hunt.

Vegetarianism

Some people refuse to eat meat, while others go one step further and do not eat anything that comes from animals. Is vegetarianism contrary to the Jewish ethic? It all depends upon the motive. If a person abstains from meat for health reasons or for *kashrut* or as penance for his sins, such abstention may well have positive value. But if the reason is based on ethical grounds—that it is morally wrong to use animals for the benefit of humans—it implies that the ethical standards of Judaism, which do not advocate vegetarianism, are inferior and that is wrong. The question is not new, and there have not been fresh discoveries that demand a change in ethical attitudes. The problem is as old as the Torah. And, since the Torah is clearly on one side of the debate, to argue that vegetarianism is more sound ethically is to be on the opposite side of the Torah.

Experiments on Animals

Is it right for scientists to experiment on animals to acquire information that can help cure human ills? This is a question that has been widely discussed in modern times. The Judaic stance is that if the experiments contribute to human health, they should proceed, provided that great care is taken to reduce any pain to the animals.

Leather shoes are not worn on Yom Kippur. Why? One of the reasons is that leather can only be obtained through the death of one of God's creatures. While Judaism permits the use of leather in clothing, it should not be worn on the day on which God is entreated to show mercy.

But Animals Are Not Human

A common fallacy is to endow animals with human characteristics, imagining that they love, feel pain as we do, or have the same kind of intelligence that we have. Animal brains are different than human ones. Animals cannot do simple arithmetic, cannot compose poetry, and do not suffer pangs of anguish over past failings. It is a natural human tendency to think of animals, especially domestic pets, as having something like human intelligence and emotions. The popularity of animal stories among children of all ages is evidence enough of this. Proverbs based on animal behavior have been held up for human emulation ever since proverbs were first told.

This tendency to identify animals with humans is quite harmless provided it is recognized for what it is—sheer fantasy, like talking to plants to encourage them to flourish. The trouble starts when worthy people, in their professed love for animals, call the refusal to obliterate the demarcations between humans and animals "speciesism" or when they talk loudly of animal rights. A creature without responsibility can have no rights. It is human beings who have the responsibility to care for animals. To humanize animals is really to animalize humans. If the vast gulf between animals and humans is not recognized, if animals are seen simply as belonging to a different species from humans, animals increasingly come to be seen as equal to humans, which they are not. Judaism urges us to show compassion for animals. What it does not do is to encourage us to identify animals with humans. That is one of the reasons why the Jewish teachers frown upon calling people "donkey" or "cattle." Even the most stupid among human beings are still different in intellect from donkeys. Humans, in the language of Jewish tradition, are created in the image of God. It is not purely accidental that some of the most notorious enemies of the human race have been animal lovers. The foul Nazi leader Julius Streicher used to return home after torturing his political opponents to care lovingly for his pet canary.

It has been noted that in Great Britain, an extremely civilized country, there is a "Society for the Prevention of Cruelty to Children" but that the organization for the protection of animals is called "The *Royal* Society for the Prevention of Cruelty to Animals." While it is important to have compassion for all God's creatures, it is most important to have compassion for one's fellow human beings. That is the sense of priority that Judaism urges for those who wish to follow its teachings.

Do Animals Go to Heaven When They Die?

It is pure speculation, of course, but Saadiah Gaon held that there is some kind of immortality for the souls of animals. Maimonides, however, ridiculed such a notion. Only human beings, Maimonides said, have the kind of soul that can enjoy eternal bliss in the Hereafter. The "soul" of an animal, its vital force, ceases to exist when the animal dies. It may be painful to children to admit it, but it is only sentimentality that one imagines that a beloved pet still exists somehow after it dies. Certainly, Judaism has no prayers for animals or such things as dog cemeteries.

GLEANINGS

A HUMAN-CENTERED INTERPRETATION
R. Huna said in R. Aibu's name: "God created Adam with due deliberation. First, he created Adam's food requirements, and only then did He create Adam. The angels said to God: *What is man, that Thou art mindful of him? And the son of man, that Thou thinkest of him?* (Psalms 8:5). For that matter, God replied, *Sheep and oxen, all of them* (Psalms 8:8), why were they created; why were *the fowl of the air and the fish of the sea* (Psalms 8:9) created? A tower full of good things and no guests—what pleasure has its owner in having filled it? The angels then said: *O Lord, our Lord, how glorious is Thy name in all the earth* (Psalms 8:10). Do what pleaseth Thee" [Midrash, *Genesis Rabbah* 8:6].

COMPASSION
Rabbi Judah the Prince told a calf being led to the slaughter: "Go. For this you were created." He was afflicted afterward with suffering because of his heartlessness. The sufferings did not leave him until he showed compassion to some weasels in danger of extinction, saying: "His tender mercies are over all his works" (Psalms 145:9) [Talmud, *Bava Metzia* 85a].

LEARNING FROM THE BEASTS
R. Johanan said: "If the Torah had not been given, we could have learnt modesty from the cat, honesty from the ant, chastity from the dove, and good manners from the cock who woos before mating" [*Eruvin* 100b].

NO ANIMAL IS A PHILOSOPHER

Someone said to a Hasidic leader: "Spinoza argues that there is no basic difference between animals and human beings." Said the Rebbe: "If that is so, why is it that animals have never produced a Spinoza?"

HUMAN DOMINION

"And God blessed them; and God said unto them: Be fruitful, and multiply, and replenish the earth, and subdue it; and have dominion over the fish of the sea, and over the fowl of the air, and over every living thing that creepeth upon the earth" [Genesis 1:28].

KILLING DANGEROUS ANIMALS

It was said to Rabbah, son of R. Huna: "If one kills snakes and scorpions on the Sabbath, the spirit of the extremely pious men is displeased." Rabbah retorted, "And as to those extremely pious men, the spirit of the sages is displeased with *them*" [Tractate *Shabbat* 121b].

ANIMALS IN THE MESSIANIC AGE

"Then shall the offering of Judah and Jerusalem be pleasant unto the Lord, as in the days of old, and as in ancient years" (Malachi 3:4). The word for "offering" is *minhah* and means "a meal offering." In the Messianic Age, even animals will become endowed with intelligence and then animal sacrifices will be abolished. Only offerings of plants, "meal offerings," will be accepted. These will be as pleasant to God as animal sacrifices were "in the days of old" [Rabbi A. I. Kook's Prayer Book, p. 292].

CHAPTER 18
The Jewish Community

Community

Just as the individual finds fulfillment in the family, the Jewish family's significance lies in the part it plays in the Jewish community, which, in turn, is part of the world community.

There are two aspects of the Jewish community: the Jewish people as a whole and the particular Jewish community to which an individual owes allegiance. There have always been divisions and subdivisions in Judaism, each with its own members. For example, there is the division of Jews into Sephardim and Ashkenazim. Among the Sephardim, there are the Spanish, Portuguese, and Oriental Jewries, and among the Ashkenazim are the Russian, Polish, Lithuanian, German, Dutch, French, English, and American Jewries. Each has its own particular emphasis, developed in part by the particular cultural background in which it flourished.

Doctrinal Differences

In addition to cultural differences are the theological: Hasidim and Mitnaggedim and—in modern times—Orthodox, Reform, and Conservative Jews. There are different groups among the Hasidim, each owing allegiance to a particular Rebbe. Some deplore these differences that, they say, tend to split Jews into a variety of sects, adding to the confusion. The divisions, however, are a fact of Jewish life and are not going to vanish overnight. History has shown that the rich variety of Jewish expression need not be harmful and can be extremely beneficial, provided that the particular loyalties are not allowed to overshadow loyalty to Judaism as a whole.

There is, no doubt, danger of rivalries that are too fierce developing among different Jewish groups. It is far from easy for people who feel strongly about their own particular views and family traditions to acknowledge that others, too, have their equally intense loyalties. The only way out of the dilemma is to appreciate that we live in a pluralistic Jewish society with very marked differences but with enough common beliefs and traditions to enable the different factions to work together in harmony rather than strife. No demand should be made that each group surrender its own insights. But neither should one faction demand that everyone else follow their particular path.

Organized Jewish Life

Jewish life is organized around the *kehillah*, which means "gathering" and represents the coming together of Jews to work for Judaism. In most communities, a good deal of *kehillah* life centers around the synagogue. It is significant that while Jews have been reluctant to call individuals "holy" (only a handful of great Jews have been given this title), they have willingly given the title to the community, which is called *kehillah kedoshah*. Individuals may be far from attaining holiness, but this desirable state is present whenever Jews come together to promote the sacred task of Jewish living. This is reflected in the social programs and humanitarian tasks each has undertaken. For instance, they taxed communal purposes and good works, attended to the needs of the synagogue and its officials, developed adequate systems of poor relief, educated the children, formed societies for philanthropical purposes, arranged visitations to the sick and the burial of the dead, and cared for widows, orphans, and others in distress.

Jewish Communal Obligations

It is a privilege for Jews to belong to a Jewish community, but the privilege brings with it responsibilities that can be heavy. The majority of faithful Jews do their best to contribute to the State of Israel, to help Soviet Jewry, and to come to the assistance of oppressed and destitute fellow Jews wherever they may be. Of course, the actual form individual contributions to these and similar good causes will take depends upon local conditions. Some contribute financially, others by giving of their time and expertise, still others by political activities. However, the Jewish community being what it is, there will be differences of opinion over which methods to use and how best to use them. But that is the price every Jewish community has had to pay.

Belonging to a Synagogue

It should be considered a high duty to belong to a synagogue and to take an active part in its work. A problem sometimes arises when one is dissatisfied with one's synagogue—should one leave it to join another more in line with one's inclinations? The general principle here is that change should be made only with caution, giving the status quo the benefit of the doubt. If there is no doubt, then and only then should one switch synagogues. However, the change should be motivated purely by strongly held principles, not by personal reasons. For instance, a person who feels that he or she has been receiving less than his or her due should take the matter up with the synagogue administration in an amicable manner rather than resign from membership. On the other hand, if an Orthodox Jew, for example, feels that he or she is more at home in a Reform synagogue or vice versa, then change should be made. But even here one should proceed with caution. Shopping around for the ideal synagogue is hardly conducive to the furtherance of the Jewish spirit of community.

Serving the Community

There is a great need for capable men and women to serve as volunteers on synagogue management boards and boards of other Jewish communal organizations. Wealthy people are to be commended for giving of their wealth and time to serve the community, but it is a gross error to imagine that the less affluent have nothing to contribute. Whether elections to positions of power and influence in old Jewish communities were entirely democratic is a moot point. The *kehillah* was frequently governed by men of means who were not always immune from the temptation to wield power over others. Nowadays, we do things democratically and every member has a vote. The important thing, however, is to see communal service as a great *mitzvah*, a real privilege like all other *mitzvot* because it is a means of serving God. Plato remarked long ago that the best leader is the one who is reluctant to assume leadership. In the Bible, Moses and the other prophets protest their unworthiness to lead their people and only agree to it because God has so ordained.

The ideal communal servant, convinced that he or she is doing useful work, will accept the role humbly and courageously and get on with the task without too much thought of self.

GLEANINGS

DIFFERENT BANNERS

In the wilderness each tribe had its own banner under which it journeyed forth. But we find no mention of different banners until the Torah had been given and the Tabernacle, which contained the Ark and the two tablets of stone representing the Torah, had been erected. Only when the Torah is at the center of Jewish life can the Jewish people afford the different banners under which they proceed on life's journey [Rabbi Jacob Kamenetzky].

GLAD TO BE US

The Karliner Hasidim have a song based on the words in the Prayer Book: "Happy are we, how goodly is our portion, how pleasant our lot, and how beautiful our heritage." The Karliners sing: "How goodly is our portion that we are Jews and not Gentiles, how pleasant our lot that we are Hasidim and not Mitnaggedim, and how beautiful our heritage that we are Karliner Hasidim and not any other variety of Hasidim."

AN OLD PRAYER FOR THE COMMUNITY

"May He who blessed our fathers, Abraham, Isaac, and Jacob, bless all this holy congregation, together with all other holy congregations: them, their wives, their sons and daughters, and all that belong to them; those who establish synagogues for prayer, and those who enter therein to pray; those who give the lamps for lighting, wine for Kiddush and Havdalah, bread to the wayfarers, and charity to the poor; and all such who occupy themselves in faithfulness with the wants of the congregation. May the Holy One, blessed be He, give them their recompense. Amen."

SOCIABILITY

"Already in Judea the Temple had assumed some social functions. The tendency first reveals itself amid the enthusiasm of the Maccabean revival, when the Jews felt drawn to the house of prayer for social as well as for religious communion. The Temple itself became the scene of some festal gatherings which were only in a secondary sense religious in character. Political meetings were held within its precincts" [Israel Abrahams: *Jewish Life in the Middle Ages*].

LEADERSHIP IS SERVITUDE

When Moses chose at God's command the 70 elders to lead the people, he saw that the elders in their humility thought themselves unworthy and were about to refuse the invitation to such high office. Whereupon Moses said to them: "Do you think it is power that I seek to give you? It is servitude that I offer you" [Midrash].

CHAPTER 19
Justice

Pursuit of Justice

The supposed distinction between Judaism and Christianity—that the former is based on justice, the latter on love—is unfounded. Judaism stresses love in full measure just as Christianity does. However, it is true that a good deal of emphasis is placed in Judaism on the need for justice in human affairs. Individuals are expected to deal justly with one another, forming a just society—an ideal not only for Jews, but for all human beings. According to the Talmudic Rabbis, "the sons of Noah" (the Rabbinic term for all people) are obliged by the Torah to have an adequate system of justice.

Justice for All

Justice is for all; no one is to be denied it. In the Bible, justice is demanded on behalf of those who are unable to fend adequately for themselves, such as the slave (Exodus 21:26–27); the stranger (Exodus 22:20); the widow and orphan (Exodus 22:21); the poor (Exodus 22:24–26); animals (Exodus 22:29, Deuteronomy 22:6–7); and even for Israel's enemies (Deuteronomy 23:8–9).

Social Justice

It is all very well, many would say, talking about the high value of justice in Judaism. But how are these great principles applied in present-day society?

There are detailed rules for conduct of the individual in society given in Jewish sources, but the majority of the rules were drawn up for a society very different from our own, both economically and politically. For instance, the rules regulating the conduct of life in a comparatively small, enclosed Jewish community can hardly be applied to the much more complicated society of today. The Industrial Revolution and the rise of capitalism brought new problems, unimagined in simpler times. The modern state is a political entity that even in its conduct of internal affairs has to take into account global repercussions. A course of action may be beneficial to the poor in the short run, but a different course of action may be demanded in order to strengthen, say, the defense of the state. It is scandalous that millions are starving because of political ineptitude even though food is available in plenty. The problem of distribution cannot be solved by a single state, however; it can be rectified only by international cooperation, which has not yet been achieved.

For this reason, there is more than one political party in democratic states; generally one is right wing, the other, leftist, each seeking both its own interests and the interests of the country as a whole. It is futile to ask for which party a good Jew should vote. In the United Kingdom, for instance, there are Jewish members of Parliament from both the Conservative and the Labor parties. Both parties agree on the need for social justice, but they are divided on how this is to be best achieved.

When a British Jew decides to stand for Parliament—or even when he or she decides for which party to vote—the principles of Judaism only come into the decision in a general way, since the issue is not one of ends but of the means used to achieve the ends. It is like deciding which medical advice to take when doctors have conflicting views about one's illness. While Judaism urges a sick person to consult doctors, one must use one's innate sense of what is just and fitting when doctors give conflicting advice.

General Guidelines

Although it is difficult to apply the Jewish principles in detail to social order, the teachings of Judaism can offer significant guidelines in relationships. Earlier we looked at how teachings concerning fair trading and poor relief can be applied in one's business and personal relationships; now we look at employer and employee relationships.

Judaism insists that both parties in a contract honor their obligations, and that applies in the workplace, too. Employers must treat workers fairly and not exploit them, while workers are expected to put in an honest day's work. These are the general principles.

Workers' Rights

A worker, anyone employed to do a job—manual or intellectual—for an individual or a corporation, is entitled to receive a fair wage. What a fair wage is depends upon the going rate for that type of work in addition to whatever agreements there may be prior to negotiations between the parties (often there are group negotiations between the representatives for organized labor and for management). According to Jewish teaching, it is right and proper for these matters to be decided beforehand by mutual consent. For an employer in a strong position to pay starvation wages is wrong, though.

Since there was no organized labor force in Talmudic times, there are no direct references to the workers' right to strike in order to obtain better working conditions and higher wages. But from the general principles of contractual obligation, it can be inferred that strikes are permitted. However, since the public is affected by strikes, every effort should be made by both sides to avoid industrial conflict. Members of a trade union should be loyal to their side in the dispute and not let down their side by opting out when it becomes convenient. As in other areas of social conflict, the individual should be governed by both self-interest and group loyalty.

Payment of Wages

The Bible is very strict about paying workers' wages on time (Leviticus 19:13; Deuteronomy 24:14–15). Originally this applied to day laborers. Nowadays workers generally receive their salaries in the form of regular wage packets so that instances of employers withholding wages are rare. Workers are also entitled to demand that fellow employees be fully qualified.

Rights of Employers

Employers have their rights, too, just as any other party in a contractual arrangement. They have the right, for instance, to dismiss employees who are lazy or incompetent or, to use a modern example, are guilty of selling the business secrets of the firm that employs them. In many countries today there are laws against unfair dismissal, and workers can take their case to tribunals. Not every dismissal, however, is unfair, so justice demands that a fair hearing be given to both sides. In a large firm, it would be wrong for a director to overlook the incompetence of employees because he feels sorry for them. That might be a worthy course for an individual employer to adopt if he wishes to go beyond the letter of the law. But for the director or manager of a firm to be too easygoing in such matters is unfair to shareholders, who are entitled to have their firm run with maximum efficiency. By the same token, it would be wrong for the head of a firm to use underhand methods to get rid of a competent employee because of spite or jealousy.

In all these matters, the good Jew should weigh the pros and cons and then decide on the course which seems most likely to further justice. The Hebrew word din, used to denote "justice," also means an "argument" or a "weighing" of conflicting attitudes. In many situations, weighing the issues involved is required if justice is to be done.

Care of the Aged and Infirm

Jewish communities have always looked after the aged and infirm. In most larger Jewish centers, there is a Jewish hospital and old-age home in which Jews who observe *kashrut* can eat kosher meals and enjoy the company of like-minded folk. To argue that this is parochialism and that there are already sufficient general institutions for the aged is incredibly narrow. When Jews look after their own in this way, they are helping relieve pressure on general society.

Perhaps contemporary use of the term senior citizen for the aged is a sign of compassion and is to be commended. But in the Jewish tradition, people are not encouraged to hide the fact that they are no longer young; old age is regarded as a time of dignity to be embraced with thanks to God. As a result of the tremendous advance of medicine, there is an increasing number of old people, which places a heavy burden on the young. Judaism urges young people to provide adequate care for the aged, since the young, too, will one day be old.

Civil Disobedience

But what if one feels strongly that the laws of one's country hinder justice rather than promote it? What if the laws themselves are unjust?

A number of Jewish sources assert that refusal to obey iniquitous laws is commendable. When Moses witnessed an Egyptian taskmaster flogging a Hebrew slave to death, he killed the attacker in order to save the victim—even though the guard was presumably acting in accordance with Egyptian law (Exodus 2:11–12). A parallel would be to kill a Nazi concentration camp guard in order to save those he would have killed. No reasonable person would argue that Jews in Germany during World War II were obliged to obey the anti-Jewish laws of the Nazis.

But who is to decide whether the demands of the government are tyrannical and should be resisted? In most situations it is extremely difficult to tell; even when the issue is clear-cut, one must carefully weigh the options, keeping in mind the harm that can be done by those who step beyond the boundaries of the law for idealistic reasons. The terrorist who hijacks a plane cares nothing for the sufferings of his hostages since he's convinced that his cause overrides all other concerns. Certainly, Judaism would not countenance the desire to overthrow society in order to build a better society on the ruins of the old. One thing is inevitable in such revolutions: the rights of the individuals who get in the way are ruthlessly pushed aside. Judaism does not accept that the innocent should suffer.

GLEANINGS

REJOICING AT AN ADVERSE DECISION
If a man's cloak has been awarded by the Court to someone else, let the man sing as he goes from the courthouse. Samuel said to R. Judah: "This is alluded to in the verse (Exodus 18:23) 'And *all* this people also (including the loser) shall come to their place in peace' " [*Sanhedrin* 7a].

FREEDOM IS FOR ALL
"Proclaim liberty throughout the land unto *all* the inhabitants thereof" (Leviticus 25:10). Liberty is for all society. It is not only the slaves who benefit. A society finds its true self when slaves are set free [Rabbi Joshua Falk, seventeenth century].

ONLY JUSTICE
"Judges and officers shalt thou make thee in all thy gates, which the Lord thy God giveth thee, tribe by tribe; and they shall judge the people with righteous judgment. Thou shalt not wrest judgment; thou shalt not respect persons; neither shalt thou take a gift; for a gift doth blind the eyes of the wise, and pervert the words of the righteous. Justice, justice shalt thou follow, that thou mayest live, and inherit the land which the Lord thy God giveth thee" [Deuteronomy 16:18–20].

POETRY IN LAW
The Torah places much emphasis on just laws. A just society is a joyous society. Jews have long known that just as there are laws of poetry, there is poetry in laws [Rabbi A. I. Kook].

THE IDEAL SOCIETY
Rabbi Kook is reported to have said that he did not know which kind of society the Torah sees as the ideal, but he was sure that it is not a capitalist society.

PAYMENT FOR WORK
Those who kept the scrolls in order in Jerusalem and the judges who decided in cases of robbery in Jerusalem received their wages from the Temple treasury. How much did they receive? Ninety manehs a year. If this amount was insufficient, their wages were increased—even if they objected—so the money they received would be adequate for their own provisions and those of their wives and families [Maimonides *Mishneh Torah, Shekalim* 4:7, based on *Ketubot* 105a].

THE EXPERTS
Our Rabbis taught that the House of Garmu was expert in preparing shewbread, but they refused to teach their skills to others. So the Sages sent for specialists from Alexandria, who knew how to bake as well as the House of Garmu, but did not know how to take the loaves from the oven as well. When the Sages heard this, they quoted: "Everyone that is called by My name I have created for My glory" (Isaiah 43:7), and they said: "Let the House of Garmu return to their office." The Sages sent for them, but they would not come. So the Sages doubled their wages, and the House of Garmu came. The Sages said to them: "What reason did you have for refusing to teach your skills?" They replied: "In our father's house they knew that the Temple would be destroyed, and perhaps an unworthy man would learn the art and then use it in the service of idolatry" [*Yoma* 38a].

YOUTH AND AGE

"Cast me not off in the time of old age; when my strength faileth, forsake me not" [Psalms 71:9].

"Thus saith the Lord: I remember for thee the affection of thy youth" [Jeremiah 2:2].

PERVERSE LAWS

According to the Midrash, Sodom was not overthrown because it had no laws. It did have laws, but they were perverse and frustrated justice. For instance, if a man injured his neighbor, the law demanded that the victim pay the attacker. A man of Sodom threw a stone at Eliezer, Abraham's servant, and hurt him, but the judge ordered Eliezer to pay a fine. Instead Eliezer threw a stone at the judge. "Now you owe me," said Eliezer. "Give the money to pay the fine." In Sodom there were laws against helping the poor; anyone who did was severely punished. In a civilized society the laws serve the cause of justice. If they serve injustice, the laws themselves are evil.

CHAPTER 20
War and Peace

Peace

Everyone knows the word *Shalom*—all Jewish prayers conclude with it. The traditional Jewish greeting is *Shalom Alekhem*, "Peace to you," to which the response is *Alekhem Shalom*, "And to you peace." The translation of *Shalom* as "peace" is perhaps too negative, suggesting merely the absence of conflict, whereas *Shalom* is a shining, positive virtue. A translation closer to the richness of meaning is "harmony," suggesting the blending of diverse colors to produce a beautiful painting. Peace between a husband and wife, for example, does not mean that either partner gives up his or her strong opinions (anything for a quiet life). Rather, it means that the marriage is harmonious *because* the husband and wife are different and yet they learn the art of mutual love and cooperation.

The great code the Mishnah ends with a saying by R. Simeon b. Halafta: "The Holy One, blessed be He, found no vessel that could hold Israel's blessing except peace" (*Uktzin* 3:12). The use of the illustration of the vessel is significant. Peace is not the highest of values nor is it an end in itself. Peace is only a vessel or an instrument by which the other virtues can be realized. For where there is strife and contention, human energies are diverted, but where harmony prevails, conditions become conducive to the realization of other virtues.

The Psychology of Peace

Philosophers have long discussed why people quarrel. Sometimes the reason is differences in outlook. The quest for peace, however, should not result in blurring the truth as one sees it, which is why the Rabbis can speak of a controversy for the sake of Heaven and give the illustration of the debates between the School of Hillel and the School of Shammai. These two great schools fought for their opinions, as did most prominent Jewish teachers throughout the ages, and did not give in to one another for the sake of convenience.

Like most things in life, the *mahloket*, the controversy, has its legitimate place. The problem is to know when to yield in a controversy and when to hold fast. Some will claim they argue because they are seeking the truth, but are merely using that as an excuse for sheer cantankerousness. Some people are never happy unless they are quarreling with others, like the man who saw two people fighting and said: "Is this a private fight or can anyone join in?" Basically, they fight because of their deep-seated feelings of inferiority. Aggression is often the fruit of an immature personality seeking to assert a worth it believes deep down it does not possess.

Causes of Contention

An oft-quoted passage in the Midrash about the story of Cain and Abel sets forth the main causes of strife among human beings. Three theories concerning why the two quarreled are stated in the Midrash. According to one, Adam's two sons, the only men on earth besides Adam himself, divided up the world so that all the land was owned by Cain and all other property by Abel. Cain said to Abel: "Fly in the air if you must, but get off my land." Abel said to Cain: "Take off all your clothes. They belong to me."

Another opinion has it that their quarrel was over "the first Eve" (in addition to their mother Eve, Adam had another woman also called Eve). Cain and Abel each claimed this woman for himself.

A third opinion claims that each of the brothers said: "I shall build the Temple, not you." Their quarrel was over the privilege of building a temple to the glory of God.

These three theories show the main causes of the conflicts that prevent brotherly love: property, sex, and religion. How many quarrels erupt over rival claims to property? And then there are the quarrels over sex—between two men wanting the same woman or two women wanting the same man. Worst of all, though, are the wars over religion, where each party is convinced that it is building a temple to the greater glory of God, not the other. If only they would see that God's glory manifests itself when human beings live in peace and harmony, not when they destroy one another in His name. Long ago, the Hebrew prophets looked forward to the day when warfare would be abolished from the face of the earth:

> And they shall beat their swords into plowshares,
> and their spears into pruning-hooks; nation shall not
> lift up sword against nation, neither shall they learn
> war any more (Isaiah 2:4).

Making Peace

This is why such great store is set on making peace between those who are bent on strife and contention. The Midrash known as the *Mekhilta* comments on the verse (Exodus 20:22) which forbids the use of iron on the stones of the altar:

> It follows that if stones that can neither hear nor
> speak yet because they promote peace between
> Israel and their Father in Heaven have been spared
> being hewn with iron, then one who makes peace
> between city and city, between people and people,
> between government and government, will cer-
> tainly be spared from suffering.

Are We Obliged To Be Pacifists?

There are many discussions in Jewish sources about when warfare is permitted and when it is forbidden. Arising out of the discussions is the rejection of out-and-out pacificism. The principle stated in the Talmud (*Sanhedrin* 72a) is: "If one comes to slay thee, forestall by slaying him"—i.e., it is not only permitted but obligatory to defend one's life against those who threaten it. Indeed, according to Jewish teaching, anyone who observes an attack upon an innocent person is obliged to save the intended victim if possible, even if he or she has to kill the attacker in order to do so.

The Just War

The Christian Church in the Middle Ages developed the doctrine of the just war—that is, the type of war it permits—and rules were drawn up to determine when a war is just. Until the establishment of the State of Israel, the decision to make war was not in the hands of Jews: all discussions were theoretical, so no actual doctrine of "just war" was developed in Judaism. However, the question did arise whether Jews could serve in the armies of the countries in which they resided. With hardly any exceptions, the Rabbis held that to be conscripted by the country in which one was a citizen was a legitimate act of self-defense.

While there is no fully developed doctrine of "just war" among the ancient and medieval Jewish thinkers, the principles behind such a doctrine are clearly stated in the Jewish sources: warfare is an abomination and to resort to violence is evil and must be avoided except in self-defense. War and aggression in self-defense are still evil, but a necessary evil—killing an aggressor who attacks the weak and helpless prevents the perpetration of an even greater evil.

But How Is Self-Defense Defined?

Problems arise when the principle behind self-defense is considered in detail. For instance, it can be argued that while self-defense is permitted, what of circumstances when it is not clear who is the aggressor and who is the intended victim? Is killing civilians allowed if that is the only way the aggressor can be vanquished? If it is permitted, are there any limits? Where does one draw the line between defense and a preemptive strike against a would-be aggressor? How do we guard against miscalculating the intentions of an enemy? In all these situations, it is not the principles that are at issue, but their detailed application. Moreover, decisions of this kind are not made by individuals but by the governments of countries; often the individual has only a minor role to play.

What religious people can and should do is constantly remind the leaders of society—statesmen, politicians, government and civic bodies, and all who are responsible for initiating plans for human betterment—that violent means are not to be used except in circumstances (fewer than most seem to imagine) where the alternative is far greater outbreaks of violence. Religious Jews should not engage in warmongering or rabble-rousing, not even on the grounds of national honor or religious triumphalism, to say nothing of class warfare or revenge. Surely by now we have learned that God must not be invoked to destroy or cripple human life, that holy wars are the worst kind, and that a too-ready assumption that God is on our side is to take the name of God in vain.

GLEANINGS

SHALOM—A DIVINE NAME
One must not use the greeting *Shalom* in a bathhouse, where people are naked, because *Shalom* is one of the names of God [*Shabbat* 6b].
God is called "Peace"; He is peace, His name is peace, and all is bound together in peace [Zohar III 10b].

PEACE AND TRUST
"The Lord will give strength unto His people; the Lord will bless His people with peace" (Psalms 29:11). The Jew who has the inner strength provided by trust in God will find peace.

WEAPONS NO ADORNMENT
Rabbi Eliezer ruled that a man may go out on the Sabbath with a sword, bow, club, shield, or spear because they are "adornments" and do not constitute a "burden" that one is forbidden to carry on the Sabbath. But the Sages objected, claiming that weapons of war could never be decorations and are nothing but a disgrace. As the prophet says: "They shall beat their swords into plowshares, and their spears into pruning-hooks" [Mishnah, Shabbat 6:4].

THE JUST WAR
The Talmud states that before King David went to battle, he not only consulted his generals on whether his army could succeed, but he also consulted the Sanhedrin on whether the battle was permissible according to Jewish law.

TAKING STOCK
What would have been the Jewish view on the legitimacy of the following:

> dropping the atom bomb on Hiroshima;
> the bombing of Dresden by the Allies;
> the Israeli War of Independence;
> the Yom Kippur War;
> or the American Civil War?

Granted that nuclear warfare is taboo because both sides will be destroyed in the process, is it morally sound to use the threat of such warfare as a deterrent?

CHAPTER 21
Ecology

The Earth as a House

In recent years there has been great concern in the world community that the earth's resources are being squandered, the atmosphere is becoming polluted, and many species are in danger of extinction. This concern by both the experts and sensitive laypersons is called "ecology" from the Greek for "the science of the house," i.e., the knowledge of how to preserve the world that is the "house" and home of the human race. The illustration of the world as a house is found in a well-known Midrash in which Abraham's recognition that God is in control of the universe is compared to a wayfarer who sees a splendid mansion on fire. At first the wayfarer concludes that the owner has abandoned the mansion to the flames, but then the owner looks out and the wayfarer sees that the mansion is in the control of its owner.

The Problem Is a New One

Although concern with the earth's ecology is probably as old as the human race itself, essentially the problem is new because of various factors which have only arisen in modern times: the proliferation of vast industries; building on a colossal scale in formerly rural areas; earth's growing population; global wars; nuclear energy; and, of course, exhaust from automobile and jet engines.

Is There a Jewish View?

It has sometimes been argued that Judaism is opposed to ecology on the basis of a verse in the creation narrative (Genesis 1:28): "And replenish the earth and subdue it; and have dominion over the fish of the sea, and over the fowl of air, and over every living thing that creepeth upon the earth." Adam was blessed in that he would master the world and the creatures therein. But the verse, and the Jewish tradition in general, does not give human beings an unlimited right to manipulate God's creation. That is why we find even in ancient times rules and regulations on the proper way to exercise control over the environment.

Some Rules from the Mishnah

In order to see how the ancient Rabbis viewed the problem in their day, we can do no better than to look at a few of the rules as they appear in the Mishnah (*Bava Batra* chapter 2). For example, a dovecote could not be kept within 50 cubits of a town, and there had to be at least 50 cubits in every direction around a dovecote on land bordering the land of others. The reason was to prevent the doves from consuming the seeds sown in neighboring fields. Since it was thought a town was more attractive when it had a wide open space around it, no trees could be planted within 25 cubits of the city limits. (Of course, nowadays trees are often planted inside a town to improve its appearance.) If a town that was being planned required the removal of trees, the town council was entitled to cut them down, provided the owner, who planted them before the plans had been formulated, received adequate compensation. Carcasses, graves, and tanneries had to be kept at least 50 cubits from the town. A tannery could only be set up if it was placed so that the prevailing winds could not waft the unpleasant smell to the town. (It is easy to see what the Rabbis would have said about chemical and nuclear pollution and the disposal of sewage.) All these instances have obvious parallels to contemporary attempts to make the environment in which people live more pleasant and comfortable.

Bal Tashhit

Bal tashhit ("do not destroy") is based on the rule in the Book of Deuteronomy (20:19) against destroying fruit-bearing trees, but the Rabbis extend it to include any unnecessary waste. The Rabbis say (*Bava Kama* 91b), for instance, that while it is the custom to rend a garment when one hears of the death of a near relative, it is wrong to tear a lot of the garment or several garments because that would be a violation of *bal tashhit*. Interestingly, the Talmud states (*Bava Kama* 91b–92a) that if a fruit-bearing tree is causing damage to other trees or if the value of the tree as timber is greater than any profit to be obtained from the fruit, the tree may be cut down. In other words, there has to be a sense of proportion. When waste results in greater benefit, it is not waste at all. As the Rabbis say in a somewhat different context: "There is sometimes a form of destruction that is constructive." That is why there is no objection for a Jew to work in demolition since the purpose is to put something more useful in the place of the building that is being torn down.

Despite the emphasis placed on not wasting God-given resources, Judaism does not encourage treating plants as if they were human beings—by talking to them, for instance. While it is a sin to cut down a fruit-bearing tree (unless it is in the circumstances already mentioned), the sin is against God who created the tree for the enjoyment of His creatures, not against the tree. It was ancient idol-worshippers who had sacred trees.

The good Jew should assist efforts that are being made for the preservation of our planet but to what extent is a matter for each individual to decide. In this and similar areas, care should be taken to avoid becoming a crank or a monomaniac. Ecology is a noble ideal, but it should not become so obsessive a concern that it diverts attention from more direct and immediate values.

The Spiritual Environment

When considering ecology, it is worthwhile to call attention to spiritual ecology, the idea that our environment should be conducive to our spiritual and ethical well-being. In most democratic societies, there is always a strong suspicion of unwarranted invasions of privacy by the government. Few would wish the state to adopt anything like the rigorous steps taken to fight poisoning of rivers or reckless driving when considering how to deal with offenders who violate moral codes.

Choosing the Best Environment

It is true that the people we live with or near have a constant influence on our character. Some communities, such as the Amish in Pennsylvania or the Hasidim in New Square, prefer to live in closed societies to protect the way of life they have chosen. But most of us do not wish to opt out of general society and cannot, in any event, choose where we want to live since many other factors, some beyond our control, determine that. Yet Judaism does insist that we strive to preserve our own way of life without being stand-offish or uncooperative in general society. What we are called upon to do is to choose friends and associates whose values are not too much in conflict with Jewish ideals. This is by no means easy in the kind of society in which most of us reside.

Good and Bad Neighbors

The Rabbis repeatedly stress the importance of having friends and neighbors whose influence is good and avoiding those whose influence is bad. *Ethics of the Fathers* (1:7) reads: "Keep away from a bad neighbor and have no associations with the wicked," upon which a commentator adds: "even for the purpose of studying the Torah." The Jewish mystics speak of an aura of goodness that surrounds the good person and one of evil that surrounds the bad. Even if we do not see it quite that way, there is much truth in the contention that we are what we are, in part at least, through our associations. The very first Psalm (some scholars have understood this as an introduction to the whole Book of Psalms) declares:

> Happy is the man that hath not walked in the
> counsel of the wicked,
> nor stood in the way of sinners,
> nor sat in the seat of the scornful.
> But his delight is in the law of the Lord,
> and in His law doth he meditate day and night.

Evidently, the Psalmist, by giving this advice, felt that the temptation to associate with bad company was acute and prevalent even in his day.

GLEANINGS

A WONDERFUL WORLD
When the Holy One, blessed be He, created the first man, He took him and led him round all the trees of the Garden of Eden and said to him: "Behold My works, how beautiful and commendable they are! All that I have created, for your sake I created it. Take care not to corrupt and destroy My universe; for if you corrupt it, there is no one to repair it after you" [Midrash, *Ecclesiastes Rabbah* 7:13].

A BLOT ON THE LANDSCAPE
The ruling of the Mishnah that trees may be removed by the appropriate authorities if the trees are a blot on the landscape and the owner receives compensation for his loss is the whole philosophy behind town and country planning. The authorities are justified in compelling an individual whose attitude concerning his property prevents the proper development of the amenities to relinquish his property for the sake of the community—but he is entitled to full compensation.

PROPER BUILDING MATERIALS
The wood used for the Tabernacle in the wilderness did not come from fruit-bearing trees. This is to teach that when we build our homes we should not use timber that comes from fruit-bearing trees [Midrash, *Exodus Rabbah* 34].

REGARDING *BAL TASHHIT*
The Rabbinic Responsa discuss many questions regarding *bal tashhit*:

> Is it permitted to uproot an orchard in order to clear the site for building purposes?
>
> Is it permitted to cut down a fruit-bearing tree if the timber will be used in the construction of a sukkah?
>
> Is it permitted to cut down fruit-bearing trees in order to plant other, more profitable fruit-bearing trees?

SHUNNING SOCIETY
"If a person lives in a land where the customs are evil and whose inhabitants do not behave uprightly, he should go away from there to a place whose inhabitants are righteous and conduct themselves properly. If, however, all the lands he knows or of which he has heard follow a path that is not good, as in our day, or if he is unable to go to a land with worthy practices because of the movements of armies or because of sickness, then he should live in solitude. Consequently, a man should strive to marry the daughter of a scholar, to marry his own daughter to a scholar, to eat and drink together with scholars, to assist a scholar in his business activities, and to associate with scholars in every possible way" [Maimonides: *Mishneh Torah, Deot* 6:1–2].

CHAPTER 22
Space Exploration

Space Travel

Eight hundred years ago, Maimonides gave a flying ship as an example of the impossible. Now, though, we have flying ships, and some of these have even flown to the moon. At first, some religious people tended to look askance at these new forms of travel: "If God had wanted us to fly, He would have given us wings." But while Rabbis were careful to warn against the risks to life in the early days of flight, they did not ban flying in the name of Judaism. However, some voices have been raised against space travel on religious and ethical grounds. It is proper in a book on Jewish ethical attitudes to examine these objections, even though it is unlikely that a modern Jewish astronaut will ask his Rabbi whether he is allowed to pursue his vocation.

Objections to Space Travel

Abraham Joshua Heschel, writing in *The New York Times* during the early days of space exploration, suggested that there might be strong objections to the whole enterprise on the basis of the verse "The heavens are the heavens of the Lord; but the earth hath He given to the children of men" (Psalms 115:16). It can be argued, however, that whatever human beings can reach is embraced by the word "earth," just as it is embraced by the blessing to man (Genesis 1:28) to conquer the "earth." Some religious Jews, notably Rabbi M. M. Kasher, have seen great significance in the fact that the moon landings coincided with the age which saw the emergence of the State of Israel. Kasher went so far as to see it as a fulfillment of the prophecy "Then the moon shall be confounded, and the sun ashamed; For the Lord of hosts will reign in mount Zion, and in Jerusalem, And before His elders shall be Glory" (Isaiah 24:23). It is extremely doubtful whether these Biblical prophecies can be interpreted in this instance as foretelling events that were to happen 2,500 years later. In any event, few Jewish voices have been raised against space exploration. Jews have tended to see human advances in science and technology as a perfectly legitimate example of the application of God's greatest gift, the human mind.

Ethical Objections

One argument against space exploration is based on the ethical grounds that it is a waste of money that could be spent on alleviating human suffering.

> Your bowl is empty, little brother,
> Your hands are blue from the cold,
> Your face is a map of terror and pain,
> Old as mankind is old.
> Men launch their miracles, little brother,
> They send their rockets up.
> But should it not be their first concern
> To fill your empty cup?
> Men try to reach the moon, little brother,
> To lasso outer space,
> But would they not come closer to God
> If they wiped the pain from your face?
> [Poem quoted by Rabbi Seymour Cohen]

No sensitive person would prefer that time, energy, and money be spent on space exploration rather than on the alleviation of poverty and suffering. However, it is doubtful whether these resources could have been made available for worthy projects if they were not used for space exploration. In our complex world, a major problem is the distribution of the earth's resources, a problem that has much to do with politics and economics. Of course, we should work for the emergence of a world in which matters are better organized. But it is hard to see how giving up space exploration is going to help solve the problem. The same reasoning applies to money spent on, say, art and music. We are not presented with the stark alternatives of having either art galleries and museums or alleviating human suffering.

In reality, the question behind space exploration is whether science and technology are being properly used. However, science and technology are instruments, and instruments are ethically neutral. The ethical question arises when it comes to using these instruments. We cannot turn the clock back even if we wanted to do so. What needs to be done is to control new instruments so that they are used in a way beneficial to the human race.

A Theological Problem

Although it is not strictly within the scope of a book on Jewish ethics, we might note in passing that a theological problem has been raised in some circles concerning space exploration. Suppose in the far future intelligent beings are found on other planets. What has Judaism to say about them since the Torah is for human beings? The little green men of science fiction are not "men" at all, but if they have intelligence and a moral sense, God, who created them, must have a purpose for them as well as for us. Is it possible that *if* such creatures exist they have been given a Torah of their own? It is pure speculation and can safely be left to God.

The Vastness of Space

Space exploration and the advances made in physics and astronomy have disclosed the vastness of the universe. We are now told that the light from the nearest stars takes millions of years to reach us and that our whole solar system is nothing but a tiny speck in a corner of the universe. All this has ethical implications for human beings. On one hand, we are able to appreciate the insignificance of man and so acquire a proper sense of humility. On the other, it is the human mind that has discovered all this and it ought to give us confidence in human thought—without which all ethical conduct would be unbalanced. The Psalmist (Psalms 8:4–6) said it all long ago:

> When I behold Thy heavens, the work of Thy fingers,
> The moon and the stars, which Thou has established;
> What is man, that Thou art mindful of him?
> And the son of man, that Thou thinkest of him?
> Yet Thou has made him but little lower than the angels,
> And hast crowned him with glory and honor.

GLEANINGS

C. S. LEWIS ON SPACE EXPLORATION

"Great powers might be more usefully but are seldom less dangerously employed than in fabricating costly objects and flinging them, you might say, overboard. Good luck to it! It is an excellent way of letting off steam."

SELF-DESTRUCTION

When iron was created, the trees began to tremble because the iron could be used to make an axe to cut them down. God said to the trees: "If you yourselves do not provide the wooden handle, the axe will be unable to function and you will be safe."

CHAPTER 23
Democracy

Democracy in the Jewish Community

The majority of Jews live in democratic states, and Jewish communal organizations are generally conducted along democratic lines. It might be considered pointless, therefore, to discuss the Jewish attitude toward democracy. Nevertheless, some consideration should be given to the way in which Jewish communities have operated in the past to discover how the democratic ideal developed. It should be said right at the outset, though, that the ethics of a democratic society are not based on the notion that the majority is always right. Majorities are often wrong. The reason why democratic procedures are favored by modern Jews is because we believe that people are entitled to be governed by whatever system they think is best for them. Whether or not it is the best is beside the point; people are entitled to make the decision, not have it made for them by those who claim to know best. Moreover, in a real democracy minority rights must also be safeguarded insofar as these are not in conflict with the rights of the majority. However, determining this issue must also be done on democratic lines, which is the basic problem of a democratic society.

Modern forms of democratic government owe a good deal to the ideas of secular thinkers, so it is futile to try to discover direct references to this type of government in ancient Jewish sources. It was assumed in these sources that a form of government vastly different from democracy would be followed by Jews. One should not ask whether democracy was envisaged in the ancient Jewish sources, but rather, whether it fits with the great ethical principles of Judaism.

In the Talmudic sources, there are many references to local government, but there are no rules on how the mayor and town council are to be elected. One well-known reference in the Talmud (*Megillah* 26a) is made to the sale of communal property such as the town synagogue. The sale, we are told, had to be made by "the seven good men of the city in the presence of the city's inhabitants." This comes near to the democratic ideal, but we are not informed how the "seven good men" were elected. Nor is it entirely clear what was meant by "in the presence of the city's inhabitants." There is no doubt that Jewish communities were governed largely by the wealthy who were prepared to give of their time and money for the benefit of the community. Being human, though, it is hardly likely that these men were always free from the lust for power or were never governed by self-interest.

Should This Be Disturbing?

It might be argued then that Judaism does not advocate a democratic form of government. According to religious Jews, though, institutions develop under the guidance of God. In this sense democracy is like polygamy. The Bible and the Talmud tolerate polygamy, but this does not mean that it is the ideal. When polygamy was banned in the eleventh century, Jews accepted that the ban was based on principles implied in the Jewish sources. Surely the idea that each human being should have a say in the conduct of communal affairs is in full accord with the Biblical principle that each individual is created in God's image.

The Totalitarian State

In addition to the philosophy that the needs and rights of the individual must be safeguarded, there is a powerful religious objection to totalitarianism. Under a totalitarian government, the state is more than the sum total of the individuals of which it is comprised. The state is virtually worshipped, and that is a modern form of idolatry, against which the prophets preached so vehemently. The Torah declares all to be equal under the law: "One law and one ordinance shall be both for you, and for the stranger that sojourneth with you" (Numbers 15:16). Of course, there are the Biblical injunctions to love one another, especially the stranger.

Apartheid

Even the supporters of the apartheid system in South Africa (in which the black population is kept apart from the whites and have been made second-class citizens) agree that the system is undemocratic—the blacks are in the majority, but even if they were a minority, some of their basic rights have been denied. But, the supporters of the regime argue, to accept the principle of one man, one vote at this stage would lead to blacks taking over, resulting in discrimination against the whites at best, civil war and anarchy at worst. It is not for those of us who do not live in that tortured land to try to advise the Jews there of what attitude they should adopt. "Do not judge your neighbor," say the Rabbis, "until you are in his position." The question of what attitude toward apartheid Jews outside South Africa should adopt is more germane. Should a Jew support sanctions that are being imposed on trade with South Africa? The debate on this continues among Jews as it does among the general public in other countries, although the majority seems to favor sanctions as the best means for overcoming the evils of apartheid.

Racial Discrimination

What is the Jewish attitude toward racial discrimination? There can be only one answer since Judaism holds that all human beings are created in God's image. Discrimination against a whole race or class cannot be tolerated. Each ethnic group is composed of individuals with his or her basic needs and rights. The color of a person's skin is irrelevant. It has rightly been said that religion is color-blind. Nowhere in Jewish sources is there found anything approaching the attitude of the Dutch Reformed Church in South Africa that it is God's will for black people to be subordinate to whites.

Racial Intermarriage

Of course, Judaism is opposed to Jews marrying outside their religion, but that is because of the religious differences. Once a non-Jew has been converted to Judaism, there is no ban against intermarriage on the grounds of color. Black Jews are as much Jews as white ones. The only ban on intermarriage even after conversion is found in the Deuteronomic law (Deuteronomy 23:4-7), which precludes the people of Ammon and Moab from "entering the congregation of the Lord," understood by the Rabbis to be a ban against marrying them. But early in the history of Rabbinic Judaism this law was made a dead letter since it was argued that it was no longer known who these people were.

It might also be added that the whole notion of racial "purity" has been exploded by modern biological science. Even though we may have prejudices, Judaism should not be invoked to justify them.

GLEANINGS

SALO BARON ON THE JEWISH COMMUNITY
"There has been a great deal of rhetoric concerning the 'democratic' features of the old type of Jewish community. Even a cursory glance at Jewish communal history must persuade the unprejudiced observer that the term 'democratic' as here applied has a meaning entirely different from that used for the political organisms of our day. The simple facts are that the bulk of world Jewry, even after the second fall of Jerusalem, was for several centuries subject to the control of the Palestinian patriarchate. . . . Although the prerogatives of the Jewish leaders, unlike those of other

potentates, were curtailed by competing powers of scholars and of individuals who wielded influence at various courts . . ., one can hardly speak of a democratic regime at any time in this long epoch."

TOO CLEVER BY HALF
Court cases in Talmudic times were decided by a majority vote, as were legal disputes among the Rabbis. The Talmud (*Eruvin* 13b) states that Rabbi Meir was so brilliant that his colleagues were incapable of grasping his full meaning. Because of that, their opinions were followed, not his.

DISCRIMINATION NO LONGER
On that day came Judah, an Ammonite proselyte, and stood before the Rabbis. He asked them: "May I enter the congregation?" Rabban Gamaliel said to him: "Thou art forbidden." Rabbi Joshua said to him: "Thou art permitted." Rabban Gamaliel protested: "Scripture says: 'An Ammonite or a Moabite shall not enter the congregation of the Lord.'" Rabbi Joshua replied: "But are the Ammonites and the Moabites still where they were? Long ago Sennacherib, king of Assyria, came and put all nations in confusion." So they permitted him to come into the congregation [Mishnah *Yadayim* 4:4].

CHAPTER 24
Epilogue

Finding the Answers

This book has been an attempt at stating the Jewish attitude toward ethical and social concerns. It has been necessary to remark more than once that it is often more a question of *discovering* the Jewish attitude rather than referring to positions already well-established. This must be so since many problems people face today are new and depend upon individual attitudes and situations. Jewish teachers are themselves divided on these issues. That is one reason why this book has left a number of questions open for further discussion, which itself is part of the process to attain the truth. Moreover, the "truth" discussed here is not at all like the answers to, say, mathematical problems, to which there is usually only one clear-cut solution. In the area of Jewish ethics, the search for the solution is often part of the solution.

Other Aspects of Judaism

This book is a companion volume to *The Book of Jewish Belief* and *The Book of Jewish Practice*. Although it can be read on its own, the subjects treated in the other two are also part of the full three-dimensional picture of Judaism. Judaism has a theological dimension: it is a religion with doctrines and beliefs about God and His relationship to human beings. Judaism has a practical dimension: it has rules and regulations about the conduct of religious life. And Judaism has an ethical and social dimension, the subject of this book. All three make up the totality that is Judaism.

The book of Ecclesiastes concludes (Ecclesiastes 12:13) with the verse "The end of the matter, all having been heard: fear God and keep His commandments; for this is the whole man." To be whole men and women in the Jewish sense is to fear God and keep His commandments. Ecclesiastes speaks of this as the "end." But, from a different perspective, the "end" is no end at all but a beginning, a summons to a worthy Jewish life in which there is room for further growth into the realms of the spirit. The Torah is never-ending and those who follow its paths share in its immortality.

Index